THE WHITE MUTINY

THE WHITE MUTINY

A FORGOTTEN EPISODE IN THE HISTORY OF THE INDIAN ARMY

ALEXANDER CARDEW

GYAN

Published by

Gyan Publishing House
5, Ansari Road
Daryaganj, New Delhi-110002
Phone: 011-47034999, 9811692060
E-mail: books@gyanbooks.com

Distribution Network
gyanbooks.com
India, USA, Canada, UK, Australia

ISBN: 978-93-7447-033-6 (PB)

First Published, 1929

2nd Impression 2025

Printed at: Gyan Press, Delhi.

THE WHITE MUTINY
Author: ALEXANDER CARDEW

THE WHITE MUTINY

BOOKS ABOUT INDIA

A PAGEANT OF INDIA

by Adolf Waley

NEPAL

by Perceval Landon

with colour plates, collotypes, maps, etc., two volumes

INDIAN PROBLEMS IN RELIGION, EDUCATION, POLITICS

by Bishop Whitehead

LANDS OF THE THUNDERBOLT

(SIKHIM, CHUMBI AND BHUTAN)

by Lord Ronaldshay

(Marquis of Zetland)

INDIA: A BIRD'S EYE VIEW

by Lord Ronaldshay

THE HEART OF ARYAVARTA

by Lord Ronaldshay

THE WHITE MUTINY

A FORGOTTEN EPISODE IN
THE HISTORY OF THE
INDIAN ARMY

by

SIR ALEXANDER CARDEW
K.C.S.I.

LONDON
CONSTABLE & CO LTD
1929

INTRODUCTORY NOTE

ALTHOUGH the events narrated in this book are to a large extent forgotten, they were the subject of bitter controversy when they happened and they involved an issue of first-class importance.

The issue between the Government of Sir George Barlow and the European officers of the Madras Army was essentially a simple one. It was the question whether the authority of the civil government was to be supreme and its orders to hold good until reversed on appeal or whether the civil government was to be liable to be over-ridden and overthrown by military force. It might be supposed that to that question there could be but one answer, but in a country so remote as India then was, and in the midst of a newly-founded empire, the decision was by no means secure. Sir George Barlow's firm and determined handling of the crisis averted a very real danger of a military pronunciamento.

When the crisis was over and the danger removed, every attempt was made to obscure the issue. It was admitted that the conduct of the officers could not be defended, but it was argued that Sir George Barlow had himself produced the very evil which he was said to have cured. In order to convict the Governor on this plea, every point in his administration, however irrelevant to the military dispute, was brought in as a support. The controversy was carried on by letters in the Press (generally anonymous), by pamphlets, by personal intrigue and by minutes and speeches in the India House and in Parliament.

The end of such a campaign was easy to foresee. On the one hand was an absent official whose defenders had little motive for ardour but an abstract appreciation of sound principles of government. On the other hand was a large body of officers who had lost their appointments in the Indian Army and whose only hope of restoration to the Service lay in the destruction of the Governor. No wonder that as time went on, and as the dangers which had been averted became more remote, the majority in the Court of Directors, which had at first applauded Sir George Barlow's action, gradually dwindled until at last in 1812 a majority was secured in favour of his recall.

Barlow himself on his arrival in England in 1813 seems to have made little effort to obtain a reversal of the Directors' decision. To accomplish that would have required a long process of agitation and lobbying which was little to his taste. He preferred to settle down quietly in the country, and to the end of his life in December 1846 he made no attempt to defend himself.

He thus allowed judgment to go against him by default and he could hardly be surprised that his reputation has suffered in consequence. Military historians have naturally not regarded him with favour, and others have accepted the general view that he was an inexperienced amateur who, in the words of the late Mr. H. Morse Stephens in the *Dictionary of National Biography*, "failed utterly when placed in a Government at a crisis."

In the following pages an attempt has been made to ascertain how far this view is correct. An examination of the history of the Madras Army before Sir George Barlow went to Madras suggests that the spirit of insubordination which culminated in the mutiny was present from a much earlier period. The events which led up to the crisis are examined in detail, and some of the incidents of Sir George Barlow's Governorship which were brought in to weight the decision against him are noted in the appendices. Although at one point Sir George Barlow made a mistake, it does not appear that he deserved the obloquy with which he was overwhelmed in his lifetime, while many of the accounts that have since been written of his career have been neither accurate nor fair.

The story of the mutiny is mainly drawn from the papers presented to Parliament in 1810 and 1811. Some additional information has been gleaned from records in the India Office, from MS. in the British Museum, and from papers kindly placed at my disposal by Colonel Sir Hilaro W. W. Barlow, Bart., C.B., C.M.G., the present head of the family to which Sir George Barlow belonged. Unfortunately all Sir George's own letters appear to be lost.

My acknowledgments are due to Sir Hilaro Barlow also for the interesting portrait of his ancestor, which is included in this volume, to the Committee of the Oriental Club and Messrs. Longmans Green & Co. for permission to reproduce the portrait of Sir John Malcolm, to the Honble. Emily St. Leger and to Lord Doneraile for the portrait of Colonel St. Leger, and to Brigadier-General J. F. Erskine and the Editor of *The Connoisseur* for allowing the reproduction of the painting by Raeburn of General Hay Macdowall.

In the orthography of Indian words and proper names, I fear that some lack of consistency will be found to exist. I have adhered to the customary spelling of the names of very well known places, while in other cases following that adopted in the original manuscripts. The word "Native" instead of "Indian" has been freely used, because it was in habitual, almost exclusive, use at the period to which the book relates to denote a native of India. It would have been an anachronism in style to have introduced the term "Indian."

CONTENTS

CONTENTS

APPENDICES

LIST OF ILLUSTRATIONS

NOTE ON VERNACULAR AND ANGLO-INDIAN TERMS

Batta: an extra allowance to officers, soldiers, etc. while in the field.

Cadjan: a strip of palm-leaf prepared for writing or written on

Country (adjective): produced in India or by Indian agency.

Dewan: the prime minister of a native state.

Dubash: literally, a man of two languages; a personal servant or dressing-boy.

Durbar: the executive government of a native state.

Godown: a warehouse.

Masulah-boat: a boat specially adapted for crossing the surf on the Madras coast.

Monsoon: the seasonal, rain-bearing winds.

Nullah: a watercourse, generally dry; a ravine.

Pagoda: a gold coin, reckoned as equivalent to $3\frac{1}{2}$ rupees.

Peon: literally, a foot-soldier, irregular or quasi-military guards.

Residency: the official residence of a Resident.

Resident: the representative of the Governor-General at a native Court.

THE WHITE MUTINY

CHAPTER I

THE BEGINNINGS OF THE COMPANY'S ARMY

It is generally agreed that the idea of a drilled and disciplined force of Indian soldiers or sepoys was first obtained from the French. At the siege of Fort St. David in 1746 the French brought with them a body of trained sepoys, and the example thus set was noted and imitated. Hitherto such Indian soldiers as had been in the service of the East India Company had been known as peons and had been imperfectly disciplined. "A rabble of peons" Wilson calls them.[1] Efforts were now made to improve these native levies. In the defence of Arcot in 1751 Clive had with him, besides 200 Europeans, 300 sepoys who fought well and proved trustworthy. The Native troops showed their value in numerous engagements in the next few years. When, in 1756, Madras had to be denuded of troops in order to furnish a force for the recovery of Calcutta, the question of rendering the Native regiments more efficient was taken up in earnest. In

[1] *History of the Madras Army*, by Lt.-Col. W. J. Wilson, i. p. 19.

B

1759 the Madras sepoys were formed into six battalions, and the number had grown to sixteen in 1767. Subsequent increases were made from time to time as the needs of the Presidency required.

At first each regiment had but three European officers, a Commandant, who was usually a Captain, and two subalterns, and there was also a European serjeant to each company. Gradually this staff was increased. In 1786 the Army was remodelled and the number of officers notably augmented. A further reorganization took place in 1796, and this gave every sepoy regiment a staff of officers equal in number to that of a regiment of the line. The Army was now divided into regiments, each composed of two battalions and commanded by a Colonel, while the battalion-commanders might be Captains, Majors or Lieutenant-Colonels.

The officers of the Company's Army were at first recruited on no very definite system. Some came from the King's service, being either transferred or recruited by the Company on their resignation of their commissions. Many were promoted from the grade of serjeant, but the defect of this class, says Dodwell, was "their unseasonable drunkenness."[1] Others were foreigners—Swiss, Dutch, German and Polish—and even deserters from the French. As the number of regiments grew and as the staff of British officers in each regiment was increased, it became necessary to institute a less haphazard mode of recruitment. A corps of cadets was formed, some

[1] *The Nabobs of Madras*, by Henry Dodwell, 1926, p. 41.

sent out with nominations from the Company in London and some recruited in India. The latter were known as " country cadets," and about 1786 the Court of Directors prohibited any further recruitment of cadets in India and declared their intention of retaining all future selections in their own hands. A commission in the Company's service was now becoming valuable.

As the Army thus came gradually into existence, the sentiment of military discipline grew up. But in such a force it was naturally at first somewhat weak. As servants of a mercantile body, and themselves often mixed up in trading transactions, it could hardly be expected that there should be the same *esprit de corps* as existed in the British Army. The officers of the sepoy regiments were at a disadvantage which was only gradually removed as the traditions of the Army grew older and more fixed.

These defects were very clearly shown in the events which occurred in the Bengal Army in 1766. Clive had returned to India pledged to carry out reforms both in the Civil Service and in the Army. After he had dealt with the civilians he turned his attention to the military. The Court of Directors had ordered that the enhanced allowances, known as *double batta*, were to be abolished. These had been given by the Nabob Jaffir Ali after the battle of Plassey, and had been continued ever since. Their abolition caused general dissatisfaction. Although the orders were at first apparently accepted, a movement was set on foot among the officers to force the Government's hand by a general resignation on an agreed date. Committees were secretly appointed at each military station. Carefully concealed communications passed from one Committee to another. More than two hundred officers pledged themselves to surrender their commissions on the appointed date. A fund was raised which was to provide for any who might be dismissed the Service. At least one of the officers in command of a Division was a party to the plot, and it was arranged that on the 1st June all officers should simultaneously resign. The fact that a large force of Mahrattas was threatening the frontier did not deter the conspirators, but merely made them advance the date fixed for the attempt. On the 6th May all officers except two in the force nearest the enemy resigned or gave notice of resignation. Fortunately Colonel Smith, who was in command of the Division, acted with courage and decision. He ordered all officers who had resigned to proceed at once to Calcutta. At the same time, he called in a sepoy regiment to enforce his orders. Clive, learning of the mutiny, also took prompt action. He wrote to Madras to send up all officers and cadets who could be spared. He announced his determination to take the severest action against the mutineers. He ordered the issue of double pay to the sepoy ranks, so as to ensure their allegiance. Finally, he proceeded himself to Monghyr to enforce, by his presence, the measures he had taken. These resolute steps proved successful. Those officers who had actually resigned were separated from their corps and made to proceed to Calcutta. The rest, seeing that their enterprise would result in their ruin, recognized the necessity of submission and withdrew the notices of resignation. A few ringleaders were dismissed. The rest were allowed quietly to resume their duty.

This attempt at mutiny was not, however, the only symptom of the tendency to insubordination which, in those early days, marked the Company's Army. In Madras, in August 1776, another event, different in character, indicated the same indiscipline among the officers of that Army. The Governor, Lord Pigott, was engaged in a dispute with the members of his Council, who resented his interference with their intrigues in Tanjore. Pigott ordered the arrest of the Commander-in-Chief, Sir Robert Fletcher, on a charge of inciting the troops to mutiny, and offered the command to Colonel Stuart. This officer was, however, in league with the Governor's opponents in the Council. He dissembled his intentions, attended a meeting of the Council and accepted the Governor's invitation to supper. But while they were driving back together in the Governor's carriage, it was stopped by officers posted by Colonel Stuart; Governor Pigott was treacherously arrested and was carried off to St. Thomas' Mount, where he was held a close prisoner for many months. He eventually died in confinement in March 1777.

These two events, one in Bengal, one in Madras, show the slightness of the foundation on which the claims of discipline and the supremacy of the civil power in those days rested. The Army knew the strength of its position and was not unwilling to take advantage of it. There existed a well-marked tendency to combine and agitate for a redress of grievances, and such steps frequently ended in extorting from the unwilling Company substantial concessions.

This was indeed the genesis of the reorganization of 1796. In 1794 memorials were presented to the Court of Directors by 500 officers of the Bengal Army, and by numerous officers of the Madras and of the Bombay Armies, setting forth their grievances. The whole position of the Indian Armies was then elaborately examined and discussed. The scheme of reorganization already mentioned was drawn up under the inspiration of Lord Cornwallis and was set forth in a despatch dated 15th January, 1796, which laid the foundation of the modern system of Army pay, pension and furlough. It recognized the claim of officers to furlough, up to a maximum of three years, after not less than ten years' service in India, and for the first time it conferred on the Indian Army the important right to an adequate retiring allowance. It was now laid down that after twenty-five years' service, of which three years might have been passed on furlough, an officer was to be entitled to retire with the full pay of his rank. With this concession, all need for the old irregular and improper allowances, which were intended to supply the absence of a regular pension, disappeared. The Court decided, therefore, that the Bazar allowance, the grant of double batta, and other objectionable forms of remuneration were to cease. They added that they entertained "the most sanguine expectation that all future causes of discontent would be effectually done away with."[1] If any officer still thought he had ground for complaint, he was exhorted to look at the new system as a whole and to balance any individual claim against the general advantage. It was evidently expected that this liberal, and indeed generous, measure of reform would put an end once and for all to discontent and agitation in the Army.

[1] India Office Records: Home, Miscellaneous, Vol. 449 A, p. 661.

CHAPTER II

THE MADRAS ARMY AT THE BEGINNING OF THE NINETEENTH CENTURY

THE East India Company's "sanguine expectation" that its concessions would immediately produce complete content in their Native Army was disappointed. It is not easy for a Service which has been for years in a state of chronic discontent and agitation all at once to throw off the habit. Moreover, some legitimate grievances remained, and others, less legitimate, were soon discovered. The agitation still went on, especially in Madras.

One reasonable ground of complaint which the reorganization of 1796 did not deal with was the difference between the allowances granted in Bengal and in Madras. Then, as now, Bengal was a wealthy Province and could afford to be liberal in the matter of house-rent and other allowances which were denied in Madras. What made the hardship greater to the Madras officer was that the cost of living was really higher in Madras than in Bengal. The matter was represented to the Court of Directors, but it declined to admit the principle that such allowances as these must be on the same scale throughout India. The Madras officer felt that in this he was badly treated.

Another fact added to the impression. The off-reckonings, a fund originally derived from savings obtained on the clothing, etc. of the regiments, were the perquisite of the officers and had always been larger in Madras than in Bengal. With some inconsistency, the Court of Directors, while refusing to equalize the scale of allowances in all three Presidencies, ordered that the off-reckonings of the three Armies should be thrown into a common fund and divided equally. This had a direct effect in reducing the emoluments of the Madras Army, and it created a very natural feeling of irritation.

Moreover, the old jealousy of the King's officers had never been completely allayed. In the early days of the Company's Army, a King's officer was entitled to supersede and take command of any officer of the Company of the same rank, however senior in age and standing. A Captain in the Company's service, grown grey with age and hard service, though in command of his regiment, might find himself superseded by some boy in a King's regiment only a few years out of school. In 1788 orders were issued giving officers of the Company equality in rank with those in the King's regiments, but the matter had not been fully settled even as late as 1807. Meantime a further cause of rivalry had arisen. Under the reorganization of 1796, every regiment of the Native Army was to be commanded by an officer with the rank of Colonel. This caused murmurs in the King's service, and in 1803 the Horse Guards brought out a warrant under which brevet rank was given to various classes of King's officers while serving in India. In 1806 the officers of the Madras Army addressed a strongly-worded memorial to the Court of Directors in which they protested against "the galling supersession to which they had been subjected" by this warrant.

There was also a widespread belief in the Company's service that King's officers were unduly favoured and given the best and most lucrative commands and staff appointments, thus superseding deserving officers of the Company. In an age when the peers and the landed gentry ruled Great Britain and dominated every walk of life—the Universities, the Church, the Bar, the Army and the Navy—it was not to be expected that India would be an exception. The Directors of the East India Company made various attempts to protect their officers, but Governors and Commanders-in-Chief (the latter always belonging to the King's Army) found the pressure of family influence and private friendship hard to resist. The petition of 1806 contained some bitter complaints on this matter.

Alongside of these genuine causes of dissatisfaction were others less well founded. A much-advertised complaint was based on the abolition of the Bazar Fund. From the early days of the Army, officers commanding cantonments had assumed the right to levy a tax, for their own benefit, on the bazars within their jurisdiction. It was an abuse imitated from native practice, but it was very lucrative, and at a time when no retiring allowance or pension was provided, there was a certain excuse for it. But when in 1796 liberal provision for retirement was made, this *raison d'être* disappeared, and when the administration of the country was transferred from the Nabob of the Carnatic to the Company, it was impossible to tolerate this old and irregular source of profit any longer. But its withdrawal was bitterly resented. Men who had been used for years to the expectation or enjoyment of the Bazar allowance were not easily consoled for the immediate loss by the hope of a future benefit they might not live to enjoy. The abolition of the Bazar allowance and the Bazar Fund was therefore a prominent cause of complaint.

The authors of the reorganization of 1796 had also overlooked one aspect of their reforms. The increase in the number of European officers in each regiment was necessarily larger in the lower ranks than in the upper. The number of officers had indeed been doubled. In the Madras Army the total number of officers, which was only 87 in 1755 and 412 in 1775, had risen to 652 in 1800 and to 1200 in 1809. There was serious doubt whether many of the young men who had joined the Army since the reorganization would ever rise above the rank of Captain. This approaching block in promotion doubtless had an effect on the spirits and outlook of the junior ranks.

Officers of all grades were feeling, too, the reaction which was bound to follow the completion of the conquest of South India and the changes which the transfer of the country to the rule of the Company entailed. A regular system of civil administration was being introduced. Civilian judges and magistrates were everywhere being appointed. The old free-and-easy ways were giving way to more formal procedure. The soldier doubtless found the new conditions irksome. Nor did it make the new system of administration any more palatable to the Army to know that the new race of civilian official was drawing twice as large a salary as the men whose valour had won the country. There might be sound reasons for the higher scale of civil pay, but it was none the less irritating, and the contrast between the rewards of the soldier and those of the civilian was a common subject of conversation and complaint at military mess tables.

The period indeed was one of transition from an era of youth and expansion to one of settled rule and ordered administration. In 1809 the Army still retained much of the turbulence of its younger days. This was fully recognized by observers at the time. Lieutenant-Colonel Malcolm, himself a member of the Madras Army and deeply attached to it, wrote to Lord Minto in 1809: "There is no man acquainted with the history and the character of the Company's Army in India, and with the sentiments that have long been familiar to the officers of that Army upon all points connected with their real or supposed rights, but must have seen with regret the seeds of that agitation that now prevails. The neglect with which the Army was formerly treated and the success which attended the efforts which it in consequence made to obtain from its superiors an amelioration of its condition, the peculiar nature of the service, the absence of proper incitements to military feeling, the want of regimental commanding officers of rank and influence, the great influx of young and insubordinate officers and many other causes have combined to produce this effect."[1] The Army had, in fact, not yet settled down to the new conditions arising from the completion of the conquest of the country. The events of 1766 and 1776 were still comparatively recent. There was still a latent feeling of insubordination. The position was charged with possibilities of danger and it needed little to produce a crisis.

[1] Wellesley MSS., Vol. 13637.

CHAPTER III

COLONEL ST. LEGER

LIEUTENANT-COLONEL the Honble. Arthur St. Leger was the fourth son of the first Viscount Doneraile of Doneraile in County Cork. Born in 1761, he had obtained a commission in the Madras Cavalry in 1781, and in the next five-and-twenty years he had seen service in most of the wars of Southern India. He had served under both Coote and Cornwallis, and in the Mahratta War he had conducted the pursuit of the Mahratta horse after the battle of Argaum and had received the approval of General Wellesley and the thanks of the Government. A gallant officer in the field, he was obstinate and self-opinionated, an intriguer and insubordinate in disposition, with no small opinion of his own worth and importance. When the Mahratta War ended he took leave of absence for three years to Europe, and he returned to Madras on the 3rd July, 1807.

During his absence the Government had created in 1806 the appointment of Inspector of Cavalry, and they had selected for this post the celebrated Colonel R. R. Gillespie, afterwards Sir Robert Gillespie, whose promptitude and daring had saved many lives during the Vellore mutiny and who had been the hero of

MAJOR GENERAL THE HON. ARTHUR ST. LEGER.

From a portrait in the possession of the Honble. Ethel St. Leger.

Face p. 14.

many romantic adventures. But Colonel Gillespie was junior in standing to Lieutenant-Colonel St. Leger; he was also an officer of the King's service, and on both accounts St. Leger considered his position as Inspector of Cavalry as a personal affront.

The Commander-in-Chief of Madras at the time was Sir John Craddock, himself an officer of the King's service. But he was anxious both on personal and family grounds to show all possible consideration to Colonel St. Leger, and when the latter came to see him to represent his grievances, Sir John Craddock did all he could to pacify him. He pointed out that as the appointment of Colonel Gillespie had been made while Colonel St. Leger was absent from India, it could not be construed as conveying the slightest reflection on the latter. He exhorted the Colonel to wait a little while until some opportunity should occur of providing him with a more suitable post, and meantime to resume command of his regiment, the 6th Native Cavalry.

Such counsels of prudence had no effect, and finding it hopeless to expect to secure from the Commander-in-Chief the redress he desired, Colonel St. Leger proceeded, without delay, to petition the Governor in Council. In a long representation dated the 17th August, 1807, he poured out his grievances. He did not wish, he said, to reflect on Colonel Gillespie, but he declared that if this officer should continue to hold the post of Inspector of Cavalry, it must injure his feelings, make him appear "in a degraded light" and lower him in the opinion of the Army. Without actually demanding that Colonel Gillespie should be removed and he himself appointed Inspector of Cavalry instead, he called upon the Government to remove or to redress the hardships of which he complained.

At this time Lord William Bentinck, an amiable and well-meaning nobleman, was Governor of Madras. He too was apparently anxious, like the Commander-in-Chief, to soothe Colonel St. Leger's ruffled spirit, and accordingly he too gave him a private interview. The Governor in his turn pointed out how absurd it would be to find a slur in an appointment made at a time when the Colonel was not available through his absence from India. He dwelt also on the obvious impossibility of immediately turning one deserving officer out of an appointment in order to make room for another. He suggested that in due time some means of providing for Colonel St. Leger would occur. In vain; the Colonel refused to be conciliated; and his attitude was such that the Governor at last said to him: "Sir, Lieutenant-Colonel Gillespie shall not be removed, as I think him the fittest person for the post. Your conversations have been repeated to me, and you shall never hold any place so long as I am Governor." Colonel St. Leger left the Governor's presence with these words ringing in his ears.

But such a declaration only increased his determination not to submit to what he regarded as supersession. Lord William Bentinck's words leave no doubt that since his return to Madras Colonel St. Leger had been talking freely of the various grievances of the Army. He now determined to make himself the mouthpiece of the officers and to ventilate their complaints as well as his own. Without awaiting any written reply from the Government to his petition of the 17th August, he despatched on the 28th of the same month a lengthy memorial to the Government of India. He was smarting, he said, "under the most severe and degrading position an officer can be placed in." From his own case he went on to the general grievances of the Company's service.

All the best, most responsible and most remunerative posts were given to the King's officers. He proceeded to enumerate, by name, six officers of the Company's service who had been unfairly superseded. All these supersessions were, he declared, in contravention of the regulations made in 1796. "The object of my humble petition," he wrote, "is to point out the degradation to which I, among the other Field Officers of the Honble. Company's service, am exposed by a system which has been adopted of excluding them from situations of active trust, respectability and emolument, while such situations are almost all occupied by the officers of His Majesty's service. Either a general incapacity must be attributed to the Honble. Company's Field Officers or their humiliating degradation is not founded on an impartial and just consideration of their services or claims." He added, not without an implication of menace, that he trusted he would receive "that redress which would render further representations unnecessary."

This petition had to be submitted through the

Madras authorities, who were much annoyed at Lieutenant-Colonel St. Leger's complaint. Such statements, wrote the Commander-in-Chief, must have the worst possible effect on the Army. They had, in fact, led already "to the revival of a thousand discussions and opened all the wounds which were scarcely closed between the officers of His Majesty and the Honble. Company's service." "I am compelled to say," he went on, "that the man most dangerous to the Army cannot evince that disposition more fatally than by the adoption of any measure that creates disunion between His Majesty's and the Honble. Company's service." The Governor was not less emphatic. Colonel St. Leger's attitude, he said, "was irreconcilable with every sentiment of the military profession." From the moment of his arrival, Colonel St. Leger had expected officers to be turned out to make way for him, and the urgency of his demands had been "most indelicate and unreasonable." When they sent on the memorial to the Government of India, the Madras Government referred to the dangerous tendency of "the inflammatory and factious proceedings" of Colonel St. Leger, spoke of the "disrespectful and injurious terms" in which the appeal was written, and said that his conduct was calculated to revive "the unhappy feuds by which this part of the British dominions was so long distracted and endangered."

Almost at the same moment another officer of the Madras Army was displaying an attitude not very different from that of St. Leger. Lieutenant-Colonel

Alexander Cuppage of the 5th Native Infantry held the post of Commandant of the Fort of Nundrydrug in Mysore. He was an officer of long service, and in 1807 he made known his intention of proceeding on leave to Europe. The Government happened to be in some difficulties as to how to find a post for Colonel James Hare of the 22nd Dragoons, who was coming back from leave and who would have to turn out Colonel Henry Davis at Bangalore if he was not otherwise provided for. The news that Colonel Cuppage meant to take leave seemed to form a convenient opportunity, and they straightway appointed Colonel Hare to the Nundrydrug command. But Colonel Cuppage, though he had announced his intention of going on furlough, meant to do so when it suited him and he was much annoyed at finding another officer, and that a member of the King's service, appointed to his post. Here was a fresh instance, it was said, of the supersession of the Company's officers by men in the King's regiments. He lost no time in ventilating his grievance. In vain the Commander-in-Chief urged that Colonel Hare's appointment had only been made because Colonel Cuppage was known to intend to return to Europe. These attempts to soothe him failed, and he presented a petition to Government so strongly worded that the Government recorded, on the 4th August, 1807, their "strong and decided disapprobation" of his conduct.

At this moment an event occurred which was not calculated to strengthen the authority of the Government in dealing with discontented officers such as

Lieutenant-Colonel St. Leger and Lieutenant-Colonel Cuppage. Both Lord William Bentinck and Sir John Craddock were recalled by the Court of Directors for the part they had played in the events which led up to and produced the Vellore mutiny. The sudden removal both of the Governor and the Commander-in-Chief was an object-lesson in the mutability of such personages, and doubtless it was not lost on the malcontents in the Army. After all, it showed that the Madras Government was neither all-powerful nor everlasting.

But, for the moment, the men who took the places of the recalled officers carried on their ideas. Mr. William Petrie, the senior member of Council, became temporarily Governor, and his Government, in a General Letter of the 21st October, 1807, to the Court of Directors, drew attention to the state of feeling in the Madras Army. "It cannot be denied," they wrote, "that a spirit of insubordination and cabal has lately shown itself among several of your officers which must be dangerous to all armies, and which, after the events that have agitated the Native Army of this Presidency, might lead to consequences of the most fatal nature." . . . This feeling, they continued, "has been greatly inflamed by the impunity with which the Honble. Lieutenant-Colonel St. Leger has been hitherto enabled to brave and insult the authority of this Government; for it is with concern that we observe . . . that every means of the most public nature have been taken at some of the principal military stations to hold up Lieutenant-Colonel St. Leger as the champion of the rights of the Company's Army and as one whose example calls for general imitation." This noteworthy tribute to Colonel St. Leger's talents as a propagandist shows that the agitation in the Madras Army was already well established in the autumn of 1807.

CHAPTER IV

LIEUTENANT-GENERAL MACDOWALL

Sir John Craddock was succeeded in the command of the Madras Army by Lieutenant-General Hay Macdowall. This officer, who came of a good Scotch family, had entered the Army in 1774 and was now aged forty-nine. A large part of his service had been in the East. When he was serving in Ceylon in 1800, he had been sent on a mission to the King of Kandy which ended in failure, and when in 1803 it was found necessary to embark on hostilities, Macdowall was placed in command of a force of 3000 men which advanced and took Kandy. Macdowall, with the bulk of the Army, then returned to Colombo, leaving a detachment of 1000 men to hold the country. But this proved to be an error of judgment. The detachment, already weakened by sickness, was surrounded by the Kandyan Army. The Commandant evacuated the town on a promise of safe-conduct to the coast, but the Kandyans attacked the retiring force, and when it surrendered, the British officers and soldiers were massacred in cold blood almost to a man. An inglorious end was thus put to the first Kandyan War.

General Macdowall's promotion was not, however, affected by this untoward incident. In October 1805

LIEUTENANT GENERAL HAY MACDOWALL.

From a portrait by Raeburn in the possession of Brigadier General J. F. Erskine.

Face p. 22.

he was advanced to the rank of Lieutenant-General, and about the same time he was given a command in India. On Sir John Craddock's recall in September 1807, the post of Commander-in-Chief in Madras devolved upon him. But shortly after taking up this office, he received the news that his position was not to be the same as that enjoyed by his predecessors. In consequence, it appears, of dissensions which had occurred between Sir John Craddock and the Civil Government, the Court of Directors had directed that future Commanders-in-Chief in Madras and Bombay were not to have a seat in the Governor's Council. This decision, though not aimed at him, was a severe blow to the pride of the new General. He looked on it as a personal affront, and he seems from the first to have placed himself in an attitude of opposition to the Government of which he was not a member.

General Macdowall at first talked of proceeding himself to Europe to get his grievance righted, but he finally contented himself with writing to England, and announcing his determination to resign unless he were placed in the same position as his predecessors had enjoyed. But communication with Europe in those days was slow. A letter ordinarily took six months to go from India to England, or *vice versa*, and no decision on the Commander-in-Chief's appeal could therefore be expected under a year. A man of stronger character would have recognized this, and have made up his mind to await with fortitude the decision of the Directors. Unfortunately General Macdowall was not gifted with much self-restraint or patience. He found himself unable to conceal the annoyance from which he was suffering. By incautious talk he showed clearly his dislike of the Government from which he was excluded. As time went on, these sentiments of animosity became intensified, and the attitude of the Commander-in-Chief became more and more definitely hostile. This was the more lamentable because the Court of Directors soon saw that they had made a mistake and decided to revise their orders. In November 1808 a despatch was sent out directing that General Macdowall, if still in Madras, was to be admitted to the Governor's Council. But before it arrived, the hasty and impulsive General had already resigned and departed, leaving behind him a legacy of trouble.

SIR GEORGE HILARO BARLOW, BART., G.C.B.

From a miniature in the possession of Sir Hilaro W. Barlow, Bart., C.B., C.M.G.

Face p. 25.

CHAPTER V

SIR GEORGE BARLOW

AFTER an interval of about three months, during which Mr. William Petrie officiated, the succession to Lord William Bentinck was filled by the appointment as Governor of Fort St. George, of Sir George Hilaro Barlow, Bart., G.C.B.

This gentleman was a member of the Bengal Civil Service, who had landed in India some twenty-eight years before. He had early attracted attention by his ability and had been the right hand of successive Governors-General. Early in his career he had assisted Lord Cornwallis in the introduction of the Permanent Settlement in Bengal. Sir John Shore, afterwards Lord Teignmouth, had made him Chief Secretary to Government when he was only thirty-three. He held that post when the Marquis Wellesley arrived in 1798, and he made himself so useful to that able and autocratic Governor-General that Lord Wellesley first secured his elevation to the rank of a Member of Council, then had him appointed provisionally to succeed to the office of Governor-General, should a sudden vacancy occur, and finally obtained for him a baronetcy of the United Kingdom in 1803.

In 1805 the Marquis Wellesley was abruptly recalled.

Brilliant as his achievements had been and immense as were the territories which he had added to the East India Company's dominions, he was disliked and distrusted by the Court of Directors, and they seized the opportunity of Colonel Monson's reverse in the Mahratta War to recall Wellesley. In his place was sent out the veteran Lord Cornwallis, with strict instructions to make peace and to effect economy. Lord Cornwallis landed in Calcutta on the 30th July, 1805, and at once set about the introduction of the new policy. On the 11th August he started for the Upper Provinces to conduct in person the negotiations with the Mahrattas, and in his letter of the 19th September he sent the Commander-in-Chief, Lord Lake, a detailed programme of his proposals. But the return to India in the middle of the hot weather proved too great a strain on the constitution of a man of sixty-six, and he died at Ghazipur on the 5th October, 1805.

By virtue of his appointment as provisional Governor-General the post thus left vacant by Lord Cornwallis' death fell to Sir George Barlow, who at once determined to carry out the policy which Cornwallis had initiated. It has been made a reproach against Barlow that he, who had been so closely associated with the enterprises of the Marquis Wellesley, should now follow a different course, but this criticism fails to observe the position in which Barlow was placed. Called unexpectedly to assume the position of Governor-General, he rightly considered that he was bound to follow the instructions which Lord Cornwallis had brought out from home. It would indeed have been both short-sighted and dishonourable to follow any other course. Moreover, Sir George Barlow may well have been by this time convinced that it was necessary in the interests of the British Government in India to call a halt in Wellesley's schemes of conquest. The state of the public finances certainly suggested this conclusion. When Lord Cornwallis landed, he had found the Treasury empty, the Government's credit strained to the utmost, the pay of the Army five months in arrears, and that of other departments in an even worse position.[1] The state of political feeling in London was such as equally to demand a settlement. "No one," wrote Sir Arthur Wellesley, "can judge of the necessity of peace in India who has not sat in the House of Commons."[2] Probably the Marquis Wellesley himself recognized this fact, for he continued a firm friend of Sir George Barlow, and wrote to him in May 1806 that he had "invariably" expressed the opinion that Barlow should be retained in the post of Governor-General.[3]

When Sir George Barlow determined to carry out Lord Cornwallis' policy as laid down in his letter of the 19th September, 1805, to Lord Lake, the Commander-in-Chief, he was, in fact, doing no more than his duty. But it brought down upon him a great weight of unpopularity. To the majority of the military, Lord Cornwallis' policy was anathema. Lord Lake eventually resigned rather than be a party

[1] *Correspondence of the First Marquis Cornwallis*, Vol. III., p. 536.

[2] Sir John Kaye's *Lives of Indian Officers*, i. 165.

[3] Wellesley MSS., Vol. 37281.

to it. It was equally offensive to the younger and more enterprising section of the civil population, who were in favour of a forward policy. "For my part," wrote young Metcalfe, then aged twenty-one, to his father, "I can contemplate universal dominion in India without much fear."[1] Mr. (afterwards Sir Robert) Farquhar wrote from Calcutta to Lord Wellesley: "The universal opinion is that this is a peace which your Lordship would never have condescended to make."[2] The odium which Sir George Barlow now incurred made his name unpopular, especially in military circles, long before he went to Madras.

An even more unpopular part of the policy which was imposed on him by the injunctions of the Court of Directors was retrenchment. Economy is never a popular virtue, least of all when it involves public retrenchment. Every man who lost a lucrative job or an allowance regarded as a personal enemy the Governor-General whose orders led to this disagreeable result. Metcalfe condemns strongly "the determined spirit of penury which is evident in this Administration."[3] The name of Sir George Barlow thus came to be associated with economy as well as with the surrender of hopes of further conquest.

In London, however, the Court of Directors were well pleased with Barlow's performance. He had both made peace and improved the finances, and they

1 *Selections from the Papers of Lord Metcalfe*, p. 8.
2 *Despatches of Marquis Wellesley*, Vol. V. p. 436.
3 *Selections from the Papers of Lord Metcalfe*, l.c.

wished to retain him as Governor-General. The Ministry would not hear of such a thing. They had no idea of letting so important a piece of patronage fall to a mere servant of the Company. They laid down the principle that it ought to go to someone who possessed "Rank, Weight and Consideration in the Metropolitan country,"[1] and they suggested Lord Lauderdale. That nobleman was, however, unpopular in Leadenhall Street. He was not only credited with "Jacobin" opinions, but was known to be opposed to the East India Company's trade monopoly, and the Directors refused to appoint him. The Ministry retaliated by getting the King to cancel the commission of Sir George Barlow and his colleagues, but they could not force the Directors to accept their nominee. At last a compromise was arrived at. The names of both Lauderdale and Barlow were withdrawn, and it was agreed to send out as Governor-General, Gilbert Elliot, first Earl of Minto, then President of the India Board, a quiet, sensible man who was acceptable both to the Ministry and to the Directors. Lord Wellesley strongly advised Sir George Barlow not to retire but to resume his place in Council.[2] The Court of Directors and the Board of Control also urged him to remain. Accordingly, when Lord Minto landed in Calcutta in September 1807, Sir George Barlow reverted to the post of Member of Council. As some compensation for his disappointment, Lord Minto had brought out to

[1] India Office Records: Home, Miscellaneous, Vol. 506.

[2] Wellesley MSS., Vol. 37284. Letter dated 25 Aug. 1806.

Barlow the Grand Cross of the Bath, and he was shortly afterwards appointed to be Governor of Madras in succession to Lord William Bentinck.

The man who thus arrived in Madras on the 24th December, 1807, was now aged forty-five. He had had a long training in public affairs. In Lord Wellesley's time he had been left for nine months in entire charge of the Government while the Governor-General was absent in the Upper Provinces. Since Cornwallis' death he had for two years himself been Governor-General. He was therefore no untrained Secretariat hand suddenly called to power. Among the innumerable memoranda in his handwriting which are contained in the Wellesley MSS. are many which show his complete acquaintance, not only with financial but also with political and military administration, minutes dealing with Native States, with the composition and assemblage of armies, and with other matters of high policy. He was, therefore, possessed to an unusual degree of the training necessary for the post of Governor.

Of his personal character Lord Wellesley wrote that he was a man of "calm judgment and sound prudence."[1] In an unpublished note he had expressed for him a "warm and unalterable sentiment of private regard and respect."[2] Indeed it is possible that Sir George Barlow modelled himself too closely on Wellesley and imitated too accurately the great Proconsul's autocratic ways. There is a hint of this

[1] *Despatches of the Marquis Wellesley*, Vol. V. p. 426.
[2] Wellesley MSS., Vol. 13719, p. 85.

in one of Lieutenant-Colonel Malcolm's letters. Undoubtedly Barlow acquired a reputation for being "cold" and unfeeling. He was charged with carrying out his policies without regard for the feelings of others, and with being "perfectly inflexible with regard to everything that he deems a principle or rule."[1] Reserved in manner and much wrapped up in official business, he did not take the trouble to please the public or conciliate those whom his official acts offended.

Although his personal character was above reproach, and although in private life he seems to have been amiable and affectionate, he was of an unpopular type, and this fact not only influenced his contemporaries but has coloured the view taken of him by those who have since written of his public career. Perhaps the fairest estimate of Sir George Barlow's character is that recorded by Lord Minto, who, in a letter to his wife, thus records his impressions: "Notwithstanding," he says, "the awkward situation in which Sir George Barlow and I are placed with regard to each other, I find no unpleasant consequences result from it. . . . His good sense and some other neutral qualities in his character have enabled him to act the part he had chosen with dignity and with many marks of real magnanimity. His good properties are of a high class. A real attachment to his public duties, and I have every reason to believe a naturally sincere and honourable character, secure his best advice as a

[1] *Observations on the Disturbances in the Madras Army*, by Lt.-Col. Malcolm, p. 65.

colleague. A constitutional coldness and apathy of temper, which has exposed him to the reproach of indifference to the interests of other men and has enabled him to discharge many harsh duties pretty inflexibly, seem at the same time to have kept his personal feelings in a temperate state and to render a second place less irksome and irritating than it would be to ninety men out of a hundred who had filled the first."[1]

To this estimate Lord Minto always adhered, and, as the considered opinion of an experienced man of the world of sound judgment and good disposition, it may be probably accepted as at least a close approximation to the truth.

[1] *Lord Minto in India*: Life and Letters of Gilbert Elliot, First Earl of Minto, 1807–14, by the Countess of Minto, London, 1880, p. 24.

CHAPTER VI

MADRAS AT THE BEGINNING OF THE NINETEENTH CENTURY

MADRAS in the early nineteenth century was a very different place from what it is to-day. Its inhabitants, who came from Europe, had reached it after a voyage which had lasted at least six months, and after escaping all the perils which that long period in a sailing-ship involved. They came out intending to stay ten, twenty or thirty years, in fact to spend their lives there. There were no cold-weather excursions to India in 1809.

The community was small, made up of the officers in garrison, the Company's servants, a few lawyers, and such "free merchants" as the Directors allowed to settle and trade in their domain. Everybody knew everybody, and people had to meet every day in business or private life. Personal dislikes and animosities acquired the bitterness born of daily intercourse. Civil servants were not yet wholly divorced from trade and a high standard of official life had yet to be built up.

As in England, the doctrines of the French revolutionaries had had their effect. Unrest and contempt for authority were prevalent among those who called themselves Whigs. Fox, the great Whig leader, had set an example of want of patriotism by his open exultation at British defeats and his regrets over British victories. The spirit of faction was rampant and party considerations outweighed the interests of the country.

In Madras the party of opposition to constituted authority found a leader in one of the Judges of the newly-created Supreme Court,[1] Sir Henry Gwillim, a lawyer of some erudition and ability, but of ungovernable temper and quarrelsome disposition. After wrangling for years with his colleague, the Chief Justice, Sir Thomas Strange, a man of liberal mind and private virtues, Sir Henry Gwillim, offended at some fancied slight, fell foul of the Government. He denounced the then Governor, Lord William Bentinck, in open court, and in such scandalous terms that the Government were compelled to take official notice of it, and Sir Henry Gwillim was recalled and eventually removed from office.

But his influence in Madras persisted after his removal. One of his followers was a barrister named Charles Marsh, afterwards a member of Parliament and the author of one of the most envenomed attacks on Sir George Barlow. Another was a free merchant named Thomas Parry, who was a great admirer of Charles James Fox and an ally of Charles Marsh. Other members of the same party were Messrs. Abbott and Roebuck, who had long been known for their open and avowed hostility to the Government, and who had been prominent in opposing the reforms

[1] See Appendix A, "The Supreme Court."

in judicial administration effected by Sir Thomas Strange.

Causes of discontent and disaffection were ready to the hand of the malcontents. The state of feeling among the military officers of the Company has already been described. The abolition of the Mayor's Court and the loss of the prestige and opportunities for peculation which it afforded had annoyed the less reputable among the merchants. The Government's assumption of direct rule over the Carnatic and the removal of the Nabobs from power had taken away other sources of illicit profit. The era of settled administration had not yet fully begun, and many looked back with regret to the licence of the past, when men like Paul Benfield could make a huge fortune out of native misrule.

Another cause of unrest was the vexed question of the Carnatic Debt.[1] The late rulers of the Carnatic, the Nabob Wallajah and his son Umdat-ul-Umara, had always been in want of money, either to provide means for their extravagance or to pay their dues to the East India Company. The bonds which they signed, generally carrying usurious rates of interest, had gradually mounted up to a large sum. There was also a vast body of forged bonds, often supported by forged entries in the Nabob's accounts. These bonds, both genuine and false, circulated freely in the Presidency. People bought them as a speculation, thinking that some day the Government would liquidate the debt. They were held by all classes of the com-

[1] See Appendix B, "The Question of the Carnatic Debt."

munity, Army officers, civilians, merchants, lawyers and Natives of the country. Even Judges of the High Court dabbled in these securities.

When in 1801 the East India Company took over the direct government of the country, it was determined to bring this scandal to a close. In agreement with the more reputable debtors, the Court of Directors undertook to set aside an annual sum towards payment of the Nabob's debts. A statutory body of Commissioners was established in London to adjudicate on claims, and a similar body was appointed by the Governor-General in Council to make investigations in India and send reports to the London authority. In order that the Commissioners in India should be free from all local prejudice, they were selected from the members of the Bengal Service, and they were about to commence their inquiry when Sir George Barlow was appointed to the post of Governor.

His appointment was subject to certain special disabilities. He was not one of the landowning aristocratic caste which then ruled England, but was merely a servant of the Company, who had risen to high office by merit and ability. He belonged to the Bengal Service, and his appointment to be Governor of Madras ran counter to Presidential tradition. Moreover, he displaced a Madras official of long service, Mr. William Petrie, whose friends had hoped for some favour from his rule and were angered to find themselves disappointed. Mr. Petrie himself shared their feeling and did what he could to encourage ill-will towards the new Governor.

Madras society was thus in an unhealthy state when Sir George Barlow arrived. It was divided into parties, one against the Government, another for it. Lord William Bentinck had not been strong enough to keep the jarring elements in order. "We trust," wrote the Chairman of the Court of Directors to Mr. Dundas,[1] "that Sir George Barlow will hold the reins of Government with vigour and discretion." "I hope," said Mr. Dundas, "that Sir George Barlow will experience more harmony and tranquillity than fell to the lot of Lord William Bentinck." It was generally recognized that Sir George was entering a region where contrary winds and storms were likely to be encountered.

[1] The Honble. Robert Dundas, afterwards 2nd Viscount Melville, President of the Board of Control.

CHAPTER VII

GROWTH OF DISCONTENT IN THE ARMY

SIR GEORGE BARLOW assumed charge of the office of Governor of Fort St. George on the 24th December, 1807. He immediately found himself called upon to deal with matters of a disagreeable nature. Within a week of his arrival he had to decide on the action to be taken in respect of an officer of the Civil Service, Mr. Robert Sherson, against whom charges of neglect and incapacity, if not of fraud, were brought forward. It was clearly proved, and indeed admitted, that Mr. Sherson had submitted false accounts involving large sums of money, and under any modern standard of administration he would certainly have been dismissed. He was, in fact, suspended by Sir George Barlow. But his case dragged on for more than half a dozen years, and was utilized by the hostile faction to discredit the Government.[1] Two months later, on the 21st February, 1808, the Commissioners sent from Bengal for the investigation of the Carnatic Debt arrived and entered on their investigation. Moreover, Sir Henry Gwillim was still in Madras carrying on his internecine quarrel with the Chief Justice and the Advocate-General. He did not sail for England until October 1808.

[1] For a fuller account of Mr. Sherson's case, see Appendix C.

The state of the Madras Army was no less disturbed. Reference has already been made to the memorial drawn up in insubordinate terms which had been sent to the Court of Directors by the officers in 1806. That had dealt with three main subjects of complaint, namely, the question of local brevet to King's officers, the nomination of King's officers to posts properly belonging to the Company's Army, and the claim that promotions of rank within the Company's service should be regulated entirely by seniority and should in no way depend on the discretion of the Commander-in-Chief. In the course of the year 1807 an attempt had been made to get up another memorial on another subject, namely, the demand for allowances equal to those granted in Bengal. A movement to this effect had been started at Bangalore, but had been suppressed. "I threw a sufficient quantity of cold water on it," wrote Colonel Davis, "to prevent its taking root and the thing died away."[1] In 1808 this project was revived. It does not appear whether this was due to Lieutenant-Colonel St. Leger's agitation regarding the Inspectorship of Cavalry or to the issue of orders for the abolition of the Tent Contract system (dealt with in the next chapter), or to some other cause. At any rate early in 1808 an address to the Governor-General in Council was put in circulation and received signatures from numerous regiments, including, it seems, at least one or two belonging to the King's service. In April it was sent to Colonel

[1] India Office Records: Home, Miscellaneous, Vol. 700. Letter dated 25th July, 1808.

Gore, then commanding the 33rd Regiment. Colonel Gore at once recognized the improper and insubordinate character of the document. He wrote in terms of strong disapproval and rebuke to the officer who had sent it to him, and he took steps to bring the matter to the knowledge of the Governor's Military Secretary, Colonel Barclay. In this way it was communicated to Sir George Barlow, who wrote on the subject to General Macdowall.

It seems somewhat curious that the Commander-in-Chief, who was necessarily in closer touch than the Governor with the Army under his command, should not have known of the existence of a movement of this nature. If he did know of it, he had hitherto made no sign, but on receipt of the Governor's letter he could no longer remain quiescent. In his reply to Sir George Barlow he professed himself perfectly ready to take any action the Governor thought proper, but he added the following significant commentary:

"Many people," he said, "are likely to view the present application (*i.e.* the Memorial) as a futile and puerile attempt and as unworthy of further notice; but my judgment and experience lead me to believe that the seeds of discontent are very widely disseminated and that almost every individual in the service is more or less dissatisfied. Every man must be sensible of the causes which have led to this position —the abolition of the Bazar Fund, first and last; the degradation of the military character from the Commander-in-Chief to the youngest ensign; the late reductions, and especially the abrogation of the Tent

Contract, are among other prominent features; and I must lament the expediency which occasioned these disgusting measures."

This remarkable utterance possesses considerable importance. In the first place, we have here the unimpeachable witness of General Hay Macdowall to the fact that as early as May 1808, that is, long before Sir George Barlow's régime could have had any effect, discontent was prevalent throughout the Madras Army. In the second place, we find the General clearly identifying himself with this spirit of discontent and alluding in unmistakable terms to his own exclusion from Council. Lastly, he shows that he had never possessed, or had already lost, any clear perception of what were or what were not the legitimate grievances of the Army, for he puts in the very front rank of the "disgusting measures" which he "must lament," the abolition of the Bazar Fund, a perfectly legitimate measure and a natural result of the greatly improved condition of the Army.

Sir George Barlow ignored General Macdowall's petulant remarks and suggested that the Commander-in-Chief should point out privately to officers commanding Divisions the impropriety of the proposed address, which was accordingly done. The letter which was sent out condemned the address in strong terms, and also reminded the officers to whom it was addressed of the standing orders against combined memorials. This circular had an immediate effect, and for a time the seditious movement seemed to have come to an end. But this effect was only temporary. By the month of July it had worn off and the question of an address to the Governor-General on military grievances was again brought forward. In many regiments officers were chosen and appointed to carry on a correspondence with other units on this subject. Among the junior ranks of the Service there was a strong desire to continue the movement. Following the precedent set in the Bengal mutiny of 1766, a "paper of indemnity" was privately circulated which was to serve as a guarantee to any officers who might suffer in the common cause. Thus by the middle of 1808 the agitation among the officers was already well established.

Lieutenant-General Macdowall, though he had in May complied with the Governor's proposal to discountenance the address, was not sincere in the steps he had officially taken to repress it. As his letter to the Governor had plainly shown, he was really in sympathy with the officers. In private conversation he made no secret of the fact that his circular was merely a matter of form and that he wished the agitators success. At his own table he openly expressed in contemptuous and disrespectful language his hostility to the Government and to its head, Sir George Barlow. Such an attitude could not fail to have a profound effect on the officers of the Madras Army.

CHAPTER VIII

THE TENT CONTRACT SYSTEM AND COLONEL MUNRO

Two years before, in February 1807, the then Commander-in-Chief, Sir John Craddock, had called on his Quartermaster-General, Lieutenant-Colonel John Munro, to submit a report on the working of the Tent Contract system. This system, which had been introduced in 1802, entrusted to the officers in command of regiments the duty of maintaining and supplying the tents and camp equipment, the carts and bullocks, the drivers and lascars necessary for the movement of the regiment in the field. To meet the expense thus involved, a fixed allowance of Rs. 952 *per mensem* was granted to officers commanding infantry regiments, and of Rs. 658½ *per mensem* to commandants of cavalry regiments.

On the 30th June, 1807, Lieutenant-Colonel Munro submitted his report. He remarked that six years' experience of the practical effects of the Tent Contract system had given an opportunity of judging of its merits or defects. He proceeded to bring forward a number of arguments tending to show that the system was ill suited to the conditions of the Army, and did not conduce to efficiency. In the course of his argument occurred the following passage:

" By granting the same allowances in peace and war

for the equipment of Native Corps, while the expenses incidental to that charge are unavoidably greater in war than in peace, it (the Tent Contract system) places the interest and duty of officers commanding Native Corps in direct opposition to one another; it makes it their interest that their corps should not be in a state of efficiency fit for field service, and therefore furnishes strong inducements to neglect their most important duties."

Finally, Colonel Munro recommended that the system should be abolished, compensation for the loss of the profitable allowances being given in the shape of enhanced batta. His view was accepted and Sir John Craddock recommended the abandonment of the system and the substitution of departmental provision of transport. This was agreed to both by the Government of Madras and the Governor-General in Council, and nothing remained but to carry out the decision.

So far as Sir George Barlow was concerned, he had had no connection with the matter. Like Clive in the question of double batta, he had merely to give effect to a decision already arrived at. A reference was made to General Hay Macdowall as to the date of the change and similar formal points, but nothing more. An order was then issued fixing the 1st July, 1808, as the date for abolishing the Tent Contract system and the allowances carried with it, and for introducing the new plan. This was a strictly formal document drawn up in ordinary official form.

The Order of Government was at first accepted in

silence. The loss of the allowances, to say nothing of the importance derived from the control of a large establishment, could not be welcome to officers commanding regiments, but there was no help for it, and the increased batta granted in compensation was some set-off. It was known that the decision was not that of the Madras Government, still less of Sir George Barlow. Nevertheless, some resentment against those who carried out the change was to be expected, and still more against those on whose advice it had been made.

Lieutenant-Colonel Munro's minute on the Tent Contract system had been written as a confidential document. It had been intended for the eye of the Commander-in-Chief only, and it ought not to have left the private recesses of the Commander-in-Chief's office. By some indiscretion, the history of which is obscure, it now became public property and a copy of the paper was circulated in the Army.

Under normal conditions, and in an Army whose nerves were in a more tranquil state than those of the Coast Army in 1808, the publication of a document such as Lieutenant-Colonel Munro's memorandum would probably have produced no effect. It was obvious that he was dealing with a question of principle, and was discussing the general tendencies of a system, not making a charge against individual officers. In Madras, however, the publication of the report had far-reaching results. It may be that Lieutenant-Colonel Munro was already an unpopular figure. His regimental rank was only that of Captain, and by his appointment as Quartermaster-General he had gone over the heads of seniors in the Service. His enemies at once fastened on the passage in the memorandum which has been quoted above, and wrote letters to the Commander-in-Chief complaining of the imputation which it was alleged to contain on their honour.

The Commander-in-Chief felt himself in a dilemma. The Quartermaster-General was a member of his personal staff. The memorandum had been written at the express desire of his predecessor in office. It was impossible to disavow a staff officer merely because he had written unpleasant truths in a confidential document. On the other hand, General Macdowall was unwilling to offend a number of senior officers of the Army. He tried to get out of the matter by an evasion. He had never been consulted, he said, about the abolition of the Tent Contract system, and he therefore did not feel himself at liberty to interfere in the matter.

Evidently this reply constituted no real answer to the officers, who found, or imagined they found, a reflection on their personal honour in Lieutenant-Colonel Munro's memorandum. They probably detected the latent weakness in the Commander-in-Chief's attitude, and they determined to press him more closely. A joint requisition was drawn up, in which the officers declared that Lieutenant-Colonel Munro's report "unequivocally conveyed a most cruel and wanton insult, as well as an injurious aspersion," to officers in command of regiments.

They accordingly formulated a definite charge that in writing this memorandum he had been guilty of conduct unbecoming an officer and a gentleman. This charge could only be properly adjudicated by a court-martial. The joint requisition was signed by no less than twenty-eight officers in command of regiments, and it was sent to the Commander-in-Chief in a letter dated 25th September, 1808, under the signatures of Lieutenant-Colonels St. Leger, Rumley and Martin.

The Commander-in-Chief had now a second chance of disposing of this matter. Had he issued a firm order dealing authoritatively with the question raised, his decision would probably have been accepted. But he again failed to seize the opportunity. Either to gain time or because he was really undecided, he referred the complaint on the 1st November to the Judge-Advocate-General for advice.

The Judge-Advocate-General of the day was Lieutenant-Colonel J. Leith, an officer of standing and experience, who seems to have fully appreciated the gravity of the issue referred to him. In a long and closely reasoned reply dated the 7th November he furnished a clear and emphatic opinion, dealing both with the merits and with the form of the question, that the charge brought by the combined officers was bad and could not be sustained. When a second reference was made to him to ask whether the defects of form in the officers' charge could be cured, he replied in the negative, but as the Commander-in-Chief seemed to be hesitating how to decide, he suggested that the opinion of the Advocate-General should be taken on the subject. The Commander-in-Chief was thus afforded a third opportunity, by the adoption of a firm attitude, of putting an end to this mischievous agitation, and once more he failed to take it. On the 30th November he communicated the Judge-Advocate-General's opinion to Colonel St. Leger, as the representative of the petitioning officers, but he added the significant intimation, that in consequence of the opinion "all further proceedings have been *for the present postponed*." It seems impossible to avoid the conclusion that by this time the Commander-in-Chief had resolved to sacrifice his Quartermaster-General to the passions of the Army. Otherwise he would never have used the phrases "for the present" and "postponed." Moreover, he now referred the question for further advice, not to the Advocate-General, as Colonel Leith had suggested, but to the notorious barrister, Mr. Charles Marsh, the friend of Sir Henry Gwillim and a leader of the faction which was endeavouring in all directions to oppose and embarrass the Government.

CHAPTER IX

GENERAL MACDOWALL'S PARTING SHOT

By the 30th November, 1808, much had occurred in Madras to aggravate the gathering excitement in the Army. Faction had been busily at work in civil society. Sir Henry Gwillim had left for England in October, but before going he had delivered another of his extraordinary addresses to the Grand Jury attacking the Government. When the Governor in Council took steps to prevent the printing and publishing of this address, Mr. Charles Marsh intervened with an appeal invoking the liberty of the Press. Active measures of obstruction had been commenced against the Bengal Commissioners who had come down to investigate the Carnatic Debt. They had decided that a certain bond put forward by one Reddi Row, an Indian official of the Nabob's office, was genuine. It had been impeached by Mr. William Abbott and other interested parties. The Commissioners believed that the witnesses called before them had committed perjury and they contemplated a prosecution. But the other side was too quick for them. Before the prosecution for perjury could be launched, Mr. William Abbott and his friends laid charges of forgery against Reddi Row and another Indian. These charges were made in the Court of a magistrate named Maitland, who was himself a holder of the Nabob's bonds and a business partner of Abbott. He straightway committed the two Indians for trial at the Sessions at the Supreme Court. The Bengal Commissioners, who saw their inquiry thus set at naught and rendered useless, asked the Government to order the law officers of the Company to defend the accused, and this was done, while Mr. Charles Marsh was engaged for the prosecution. The trial took place before the Chief Justice. Sir Thomas Strange summed up strongly in favour of the accused, but the jury found them guilty. Sir Thomas Strange so strongly believed this to be a perverse verdict that he refused to pass sentence, and finally referred the case to the Crown and got the conviction quashed. Meantime the anti-government faction presented Mr. Marsh with an address eulogizing him for his fearless defence of the rights of juries. Everybody took sides in the dispute, and one of the people who signed the address to Mr. Marsh was Captain Josiah Marshall, Secretary to the Military Board and an intimate friend of General Macdowall.[1]

A year had now elapsed since the General had applied to the Court of Directors to give him the same status, a seat in the Governor's Council, as his predecessors had enjoyed. As we have noticed, it had actually been determined in England to grant this request, but the orders did not reach Madras until some time later. Meantime the Commander-in-

[1] For a fuller account of the Carnatic Debt Question, see Appendix B.

Chief's exasperation had reached a point at which it could no longer be controlled. In November 1808 he tendered his resignation to the Governor-General, thus trying to ignore the local Government. On the 5th December he was told that if he resigned, it must be to the Government of Madras.

The General was at this time absent from Madras on a long tour in the Northern Districts of the Presidency. On the 24th December he was at Masulipatam. There he reviewed the European regiment and delivered an address to the soldiers, which appears to have been directly intended to promote discontent and disaffection. He told them that the regiment had been overlooked, in fact neglected, and he left them to infer that this neglect was not his fault but that of the Government. It seems fair to conclude, from this recorded address, that the Commander-in-Chief used similar language elsewhere. Early in January he gave further proof of his state of mind. He forwarded to Government for transmission to the Court of Directors the very memorial whose submission in the previous May he had prohibited. This memorial had indeed been made far more comprehensive and aggressive. It began by referring to the abolition of the Bazar allowance and of double batta to officers commanding outposts. These, said the memorial, "we have been taught from our first entering the Service to look on as our inalienable rights." The paper then went on to complain of the preference shown to the King's officers, of the higher allowances granted in Bengal, and of the recent abolition of the Tent Contract allowance, with a passing allusion to the "base and unfounded insinuations" by which that abolition had been supported. Lastly, the memorial commented on the grievance caused to the Army by the Commander-in-Chief's exclusion from Council.

The submission of this collective memorial by the officers of the Army was a serious infraction of discipline and a contravention of the orders to which the Commander-in-Chief had himself drawn attention in May 1808. The reference to old abuses, such as the bazar allowance, as among "the inalienable rights" of the Army, proved how largely a spirit of faction actuated the memorialists. Had the Commander-in-Chief retained at this date any sense of propriety and any sound judgment of facts, he would have refused to send on the memorial. Instead of that, he not only sent it on but he supported it and praised its "studied moderation." Ignoring the extraordinarily liberal provisions under which officers were now enabled to retire on full pay after twenty-five years' service, he told the Government that the Army had gradually seen "the annihilation of every emolument that could afford present comfort or have held out, though at a remote period, a prospect of future competency."

While General Macdowall was thus supporting, so far as lay in his power, the unreasonable and irregular representations of the general body of officers, he also lent countenance to the hardly less improper petitions of an individual officer. Lieutenant-Colonel St. Leger was again to the fore with a grievance. Four troops of his regiment had been sent to Persia, and two were under orders for Travancore, and he asked to know why he had not himself been deemed worthy to command them in the field. He urged, not without reason, that it seemed like a reflection on him to leave him with only a troop or two at the depôt, and with characteristic vehemence he demanded to be brought before a court-martial to ascertain why he had been placed "in so degrading and unprecedented a position." The Commander-in-Chief was evidently not displeased at the opening given him by this memorial, which he described as "a candid and moderate appeal." He expressed his sympathy with Lieutenant-Colonel St. Leger, who had been placed, he said, "in a most cruel predicament." At the same time he strongly urged that Lieutenant-Colonel St. Leger should be given the command of the force that was about to operate against Travancore. He solemnly pledged himself that Colonel St. Leger, if appointed, would prove a success and would "do credit to his character and that honour to his country which has been inherent in his family since the days of William the Norman."

The proposed operations against Travancore had already been the subject of many acrimonious letters from the Commander-in-Chief to the Chief Secretary. General Macdowall complained of his not having been consulted regarding the composition of the force and other details. It was explained to him that the expedition was an urgent matter and had been determined on when he was absent from Madras and in a remote part of the Presidency; that full copies of all papers had been sent to him; and that, on his return to Madras, the Chief Secretary had been sent to wait on him at his residence with all the latest papers. None of these explanations had any effect, nor did the action of the Governor in complying with General Macdowall's recommendation and appointing Lieutenant-Colonel St. Leger to command the force which was to advance on the eastern boundary of Travancore have any better result.

On the 15th January Lieutenant-General Macdowall sent in a definite announcement of his intention to resign the office of Commander-in-Chief. This paper was more in the nature of a manifesto than an ordinary letter. It recited, at considerable length, the General's grievances. The decision of the Directors to exclude him from Council had, he said, placed him "in so extraordinary, so unexampled, and so humiliating a predicament as to excite in him the most painful emotions." After sixteen months' trial of the position he had determined to bear it no longer. "By adhering rigidly," he went on, "to a point of honour, my prospects in life may be materially affected, but I am resolved that my name shall not be branded with the reproach of having been the first General Officer who retained a situation after all hope of restoration to its former distinction had expired. . . . I have been offered an indignity, and my pride and sensibility would compel me to retire, even were the sacrifice greater, for I cannot tamely submit to see the exalted station disgraced in my person, nor can I be answerable to the Army if I do not resist so uncommon a deviation which deprives it of a representative in Council."

Lieutenant-General Macdowall was not content with this letter to the Governor in Council. He felt it necessary also to proclaim his injured feelings to the Army. In a farewell address he laid bare to the officers the full extent of his discontent. "Had Lieutenant-General Macdowall," ran the address, "succeeded to the high and enviable office (of Commander-in-Chief) with all the advantages enjoyed by his predecessors, he would, upon first assuming the command, have promulgated his sentiments on so flattering an event. But the circumstances of his appointment were so humiliating and unpropitious that he declined addressing the Army in the anxious hope that the Court of Directors might, on further deliberation, be induced to restore him to his rights, and, by altering the new and extraordinary form of Government, have enabled him to exercise the functions of his station, as the representative of the Army, with honour to the Service and with credit to himself; no prospect of such an occurrence appearing at all, in justice to the Army, and to his character, he has determined to retire." A public declaration of this sort, addressed to the officers who were already labouring under much excitement, was plainly a dangerous proceeding, and fully merits Lieutenant-Colonel Malcolm's comparison of it to a man waving a torch over a powder magazine.

Worse, however, was to follow. Since the 30th November, 1808, when General Macdowall had told

Lieutenant-Colonel St. Leger that all proceedings against Lieutenant-Colonel Munro were "for the present postponed," a steady agitation against the Quartermaster-General had been kept up by the malcontent officers. On the 12th December, Lieutenant-Colonel George Martin had put in a lengthy reply to the opinion of the Advocate-General, in which he had even argued that Munro had written his note on the Tent Contract question not in his official capacity but as a private individual! A little later the officers who were banded together in this matter put in a fresh paper, withdrawing their request for a court-martial, because the Advocate-General had declared it inadmissible, and appealing to the Court of Directors to deal with Munro.

The Commander-in-Chief still hesitated. The date of his departure was approaching and he had given no decision, although he had now received Mr. Charles Marsh's opinion. So late as the 20th January he saw Lieutenant-Colonel Munro, and personally told him that he meant to leave the matter to be dealt with by his successor. A few hours later he changed his mind, for reasons which are now unknown, and he sent an official order to the Quartermaster-General placing him under arrest with a view to his being brought before a court-martial. A request for reconsideration was rejected, the reason assigned being that he could not leave so troublesome a matter to be dealt with by an incoming Commander-in-Chief. Lieutenant-Colonel George Martin was appointed to conduct the prosecution.

Lieutenant-Colonel Munro thus found himself, a

week before General Macdowall was to leave India, abandoned to his enemies. Only one course was left open to him, if he was not to be subjected to the ignominy of a court-martial. He drew up an appeal to the Governor in Council and sent it to the Commander-in-Chief for transmission. This step greatly increased the General's anger. On the 23rd January he declared that he regarded Lieutenant-Colonel Munro's conduct as "extremely indelicate and disrespectful," and he refused to forward the appeal on the ground that his order related to a court-martial, which was a purely military matter, and with which the Governor in Council had no power to interfere. Lieutenant-Colonel Munro then sent his appeal direct to the Government.

The first action Sir George Barlow took was to consult his legal advisers. The appeal was referred to the Advocate-General, who was told to reply after consulting the Judge-Advocate-General. The opinion of these officers was soon given. The impropriety of subjecting to a court-martial an officer in the position of Quartermaster-General for expressions used in a confidential memorandum written on a privileged occasion was obvious. Moreover, Lieutenant-Colonel Munro's advice had been accepted and acted on by the Government. To bring him before a court-martial for such advice was tantamount to an arraignment of the Governor in Council. On both grounds it was felt that Lieutenant-Colonel Munro ought to be protected. The Statute gave general control in all military matters to the Governor in Council, and it was decided to intervene. On the

24th January the Government wrote to the Commander-in-Chief "suggesting in the most earnest manner," that, as Lieutenant-Colonel Munro's act was really now the act of Government, the order for a court-martial should be reconsidered and Munro released from arrest.

Under normal conditions such a representation might have been expected to succeed, but the Commander-in-Chief had burnt his boats and could not turn back. He returned a heated reply, saying that he regarded the letter of the Governor in Council as "an implied censure of his conduct as Commander-in-Chief," and declaring that he could not alter his decision "without compromising the honour of the whole Army." He went on to add that he should now frame an additional charge against Lieutenant-Colonel Munro, namely, that of having shown disrespect to the Commander-in-Chief by presuming to appeal from him to the Governor in Council.

This letter constituted so direct a challenge to the supremacy of the Government that there was no option but to take it up. On the 27th January the Governor in Council replied. General Macdowall was called upon to state definitely whether he intended to comply with the Government's orders on the subject of the release of the Quartermaster-General from arrest. To this the Commander-in-Chief answered that he could not yield up his military authority without a protest, but if the Government persisted in issuing a positive order for the release of Lieutenant-Colonel Munro, he must, of course, submit. He added that "by this act the degradation of the Commander-in-

Chief will be completed." On the same day the Government issued orders peremptorily ordering the release of Munro from arrest, and the instruction was obeyed.

The order of the Government reached Lieutenant-General Macdowall on Saturday the 28th January, 1809. He was sailing for England the next day. He had not yet technically given up the post of Commander-in-Chief. This was usually deferred till the departing official reached the last port in the Presidency at which his ship would touch. On the Saturday a General Order addressed to the Army was hastily prepared. It was in the following terms:

> "The immediate departure of Lieutenant-General Macdowall from Madras will prevent his pursuing the design of bringing Lieutenant-Colonel Munro, Quartermaster-General, to trial for disrespect to the Commander-in-Chief, for disobedience of orders, and for contempt of military authority in having resorted to the power of the Civil Government in defiance of the judgment of the officer at the head of the Army, who had placed him under arrest on charges preferred against him by a number of officers commanding native corps; in consequence of which appeal direct to the Honble. the President in Council, Lieutenant-General Macdowall has received a positive order from the Chief Secretary to liberate Lieutenant-Colonel Munro from arrest. Such conduct on the part of Lieutenant-Colonel Munro being destructive of subordination, sub-

versive of military discipline, a violation of the sacred rights of the Commander-in-Chief, and holding out a most dangerous example to the Service, Lieutenant-General Macdowall, in support of the dignity of the profession and of his own station and character, feels it incumbent on him to express his strong disapprobation of Lieutenant-Colonel Munro's unexampled proceedings, and considers it a solemn duty imposed upon him to reprimand Lieutenant-Colonel Munro in General Orders, and he is hereby reprimanded accordingly."

This order was copied in hot haste on Saturday afternoon. It was despatched in manuscript the same night—Saturday—to the principal military stations. Next day printed copies were obtained, and in spite of its being Sunday, Major Boles, the Deputy-Adjutant-General, attended office and signed further copies for despatch. That afternoon, Lieutenant-General Hay Macdowall, having, by his rash and ill-considered proceedings, done the very utmost in his power to inflame the already agitated Army of Madras, embarked for England. The General was not, however, destined to reach home, for his ship, the *Lady Jane Dundas*, was lost with all hands somewhere near the Cape.[1] He did not live to see the serious results of his conduct in Madras, nor is his explanation of his actions on record. But he cannot, therefore, be exempt from criticism and responsibility.

[1] Some of the last letters from this unfortunate officer are printed in Appendix D.

CHAPTER X

THE GOVERNMENT'S BLUNDER

Up to this point Sir George Barlow had acted with restraint and discretion. When General Hay Macdowall made complaints of not being consulted sufficiently on military matters, he was answered in a temperate manner and was given explanations which were generally adequate. When he pressed upon the Governor Lieutenant-Colonel St. Leger's claims to be given a command in the expedition against Travancore, Sir George Barlow at once complied with the Commander-in-Chief's wishes and appointed St. Leger to command the force moving from Trichinopoly. In a similar manner, on Lieutenant-Colonel St. Leger's complaint that his regiment had received no thanks from the Government for its alacrity in providing several troops for service in Persia, an order of suitable acknowledgment was at once published. No notice was taken of General Macdowall's petulant remarks in his letter of resignation, and his farewell address to the Army was also allowed to pass unnoticed. The Government's intervention on behalf of Lieutenant-Colonel Munro was undertaken to save an innocent man from a malicious prosecution. It was forced on the Government by the infatuated proceedings of General Macdowall, and few unbiassed judges would hold that in the circumstances it was not justified.

Unfortunately, at this juncture Sir George Barlow's self-restraint gave way. As soon as the Commander-in-Chief's General Order reached the Government on Monday, the 30th January, it was resolved to recall the fleet, which was not yet out of sight, and guns were fired from the fort with this object, but this endeavour failed. Other measures of retaliation were therefore resolved upon. With haste nearly as great and as unwise as that of General Macdowall, an Order of Government was prepared and was issued next day, the 31st January. After condemning in strong terms the Commander-in-Chief's action, it declared that though he had set sail, he had not yet resigned. For the purpose of preventing the possible repetition of further acts of outrage, said the Order, General Macdowall was removed from the post of Commander-in-Chief. His General Order of the 28th January was directed to be expunged from every public record. Finally, it was declared that Major Thomas Boles, Deputy-Adjutant-General, whose signature appeared at the foot of the Order, was suspended from the Service until the pleasure of the Court of Directors should be known. The following day Lieutenant-Colonel F. Capper, the Adjutant-General, was likewise suspended.

It is quite possible to hold that the punishment thus inflicted on General Macdowall was justified. His action in publicly censuring Lieutenant-Colonel Munro for appealing to the Governor in Council conveyed, and doubtless was meant to convey, a censure on the Government itself. This was a grossly improper proceeding and called for some prompt notice, although, as the Commander-in-Chief had already set sail and no further " outrages " were really likely, his removal from office was hardly necessary.

But the suspension of Major Boles falls into a different category. Major Boles, like Lieutenant-Colonel Munro, on whose behalf the Government had just intervened, was merely a ministerial officer. In placing his signature to an order drawn up by his superior officer, the Commander-in-Chief, he was performing a purely ministerial act. Every such signature purports and is perfectly known to be affixed merely " by order." It does not import that the officer who signs the paper has any responsibility for its contents, of which he may wholly disapprove. To suspend Major Boles for signing an order in the ordinary scope of his duty and in obedience to the instructions of the Commander-in-Chief was a patent act of injustice.

Attempts were afterwards made to defend this blunder on two grounds. In the first place it was declared that it was essential to show that a military officer who obeys an *illegal* command of his superior is not protected. Lieutenant-Colonel Leith, the Judge-Advocate-General, gave the Government an opinion to this effect, and we find Sir George Barlow writing to the Governor-General that the punishment of Major Boles was necessary to establish this principle.[1] But it is hardly necessary to point out that in this case the principle did not arise. The Commander-in-Chief's

[1] India Office Records: Home, Miscellaneous, Vol. 695.

order, however grave a breach of decorum, was not illegal, nor was his order to sign it. The second ground on which the suspension of Major Boles was sought to be defended was equally inadequate. It was said that under an old rule no General Order was to be issued to the Army until it had first been sent to the Government. But it was satisfactorily proved that if such a rule existed (which was doubtful) it had been in desuetude for many years, and that it was not customary to withhold General Orders until twenty-four hours after they had been dispatched to the Government. The defence of the suspension of Major Boles therefore fails on both points.

In fact few can doubt that the suspension of Major Boles was an arbitrary act undertaken under the influence of anger. Sir George Barlow, justly irritated by the manifesto of the departing Commander-in-Chief, unjustly struck at all who were connected with that document. By this single error of judgment he put himself in the wrong and adopted a false position from which he could not afterwards retreat. No clearer illustration of the evils inherent both in autocratic power and in surrender to the passions was ever presented.

CHAPTER XI

INCREASING TENSION IN THE ARMY

THE appointment of Commander-in-Chief, which Lieutenant-General Macdowall's removal had left vacant, was conferred upon Major-General Francis Gowdie. This officer, who belonged to the East India Company's service, seems to have been a man of amiable disposition, if not of very great strength of character. Colonel Welsh, who knew him at Madura in 1794, describes him there as "kind and considerate to all, hospitable, the father in the community."[1] Had he been Commander-in-Chief a year earlier, it is possible that there would have been no excitement in the Army and no mutiny. But he was not apparently a man of strong personality. Lord Minto refers to him in slighting terms, and he seems soon to have been regarded as a mere instrument for carrying out Sir George Barlow's decrees.

The first step taken by the Government after General Gowdie's appointment was in the direction of appeasement of the military excitement. In an order dated 6th February the proceedings connected with Lieutenant-Colonel Munro's case were reviewed. In conciliatory terms, the Government declared that

[1] *Military Reminiscences*, by Colonel James Welsh, 2 Vols., 1830, p. 23.

they were as anxious as anyone to guard the honour of the Army. They had, therefore, carefully considered the memorandum which Lieutenant-Colonel Munro had written in 1807, and they were convinced that it was impossible, under any reasonable interpretation, to attach any offensive meaning to his words. They hoped, therefore, that the matter of that paper would now be allowed to drop.

This order failed to produce the desired effect. The friends and followers of General Macdowall had already set to work to develop the agitation which his removal had excited. A small body of officers of the Headquarter Staff, Colonel Capper, the suspended Adjutant-General, Captain Josiah Marshall, Secretary to the Military Board, who had signed the address to Mr. Marsh, his Deputy, Lieutenant Stock, Captain J. M. Coombs, the late Commander-in-Chief's Aide-de-Camp, and Lieutenant-Colonel Martin, who had taken so prominent a part in the attack on Munro, seem to have been the leaders. They drew up in secret conclave a memorial to the Governor-General, in which, after referring to the exclusion of the Commander-in-Chief from a seat in Council, they spoke of the Government's intervention in the case of Colonel Munro as "a dangerous innovation and infringement of the solemn laws of the Army." They said that by the removal of General Macdowall and the suspension of Colonel Capper and Major Boles, "the exclusive rights of the army had been violated," and they begged the Supreme Government "to anticipate the extreme crisis of their agitation" by releasing them from the control of a ruler whose measures were as detrimental to the State as they were repulsive to the feelings of a loyal and patriotic Army.

This memorial was undoubtedly of a seditious character. It exhibited the Army as demanding the removal of the Governor of the Presidency, and conveying the threat that if their demands were not complied with, if " the extreme crisis of their agitation " were not anticipated, they would take the law into their own hands. The document was, in fact, a warning of mutiny.

At the same time an address was prepared to Major Boles, condoling with him on his " severe and unmerited punishment," and proposing to repair his injuries by subscribing the full amount of his pay and staff allowance. Copies of these papers were taken by Colonel Capper to Colombo, where he met and accompanied General Macdowall in the ill-fated *Lady Jane Dundas*. Other copies were circulated for signature in the Presidency town, while others again were sent to the Army in Travancore and to all military stations and cantonments. Arrangements were made to collect subscriptions for Major Boles and to remit them to him. All this was carried on with as much secrecy as possible.

Before long, however, rumours of what was going on began to reach Government and the new Commander-in-Chief. On the 5th March General Gowdie sent a circular letter to officers in command of Divisions telling them that he had heard of improper memorials and addresses being in circulation, and warning them to suppress any such papers. Most of the officers replied assuring the Commander-in-Chief that they had heard of no such documents and would repress them if they did, but one, namely, Colonel John Cuppage, sent a reply couched in ambiguous tones, and Major de Morgan wrote from Tellicherry in terms which seemed clearly to contain a defiance of the Government. Meantime inquiries had been set on foot in Madras to find out who were the authors of the objectionable papers. The clerks of the Military offices were examined by the Advocate-General in the presence of the Governor, and no great difficulty was experienced in discovering who were the persons concerned.

Information also began to come in regarding the circulation of the documents in the Army, and this at once showed that Lieutenant-Colonel St. Leger was implicated. The force of which he had been given the command had moved from Trichinopoly against Travancore in January, and in less than a month had reached all its objectives. There was, in fact, little serious opposition. The Diwan, who was the cause of the trouble, fled, and the Durbar submitted. "The enemy," wrote Colonel James Welsh, who bore an important part in the operations, "proved far below our expectations." Colonel St. Leger's task was not actually a very arduous one, but the Government had issued a very handsome acknowledgment of the services of him and his troops.

Neither this order, nor the compliment paid him in the bestowal of the command, had, however, been sufficient to conciliate Colonel St. Leger. The agitation in the Army was indeed facilitated by the concentration of a considerable number of regiments in Travancore. "An officer of rank and character" is quoted by Lord Minto as having written about this time on the subject of the memorial: "It was brought to me by Colonel St. Leger for signature. I pointed out that in place of being of any service to General Macdowall, it would forcibly impress on the minds of all thinking people the dangerous, not to say mutinous, spirit he excited in the Army against the very Government it was their bounden duty to support. But they have a strange jumbled idea of military subordination; they talk of their rights as they would of a landed property secured to them by a legal grant." Lieutenant-Colonel W. Macleod of His Majesty's 69th Regiment subsequently testified that while he was serving under Colonel St. Leger in Travancore, the latter called on him with the memorial to read and sign, if he approved. Colonel Macleod refused to sign, but he had heard that 400 officers of the Army in Travancore had signed the paper. There was other evidence to show that Colonel St. Leger had taken a leading part in fomenting the agitation, although the memorial was never actually despatched.

News of these doings naturally reached Madras, and on the 7th April a letter was despatched to the Resident in Travancore, instructing him to relieve Colonel St. Leger of his command and to order him to return to the headquarters of his regiment at Trichinopoly. In this communication, either by accident or design, Colonel St. Leger was referred to without the customary prefix "the Honourable." He immediately assumed that the omission was intentional, and he wrote an angry letter to the Government dated the 27th April. "Although," he said, "it may be in the power of the Honble. the Governor in Council to wound my feelings and to degrade me from my command, I am ignorant of any power or authority vested in him to annul the title to which my birth has elevated me." This protest against the carelessness or discourtesy of the Government's communication might well have been excused, but Lieutenant-Colonel St. Leger then proceeded to retaliate by giving his opinion on the treatment dealt out to Major Boles, a matter in which he was certainly not called upon to intervene. If Major Boles, he said, had refused to sign the late Commander-in-Chief's General Order he would have deserved to be court-martialled for such refusal, and had Lieutenant-Colonel St. Leger been a member of such a court-martial, he would have awarded no punishment less than dismissal from the Service as a penalty for such disobedience. The inference from these remarks was clear. The Government, in punishing Major Boles, had punished a man for doing what was merely his plain duty. Whether this was true or not, Lieutenant-Colonel St. Leger's action in writing these remarks was not the less a breach of discipline and decorum and a defiance of the Government to which he was subordinate.

CHAPTER XII

THE ACTION OF THE GOVERNMENT

THE Government was by this time faced with a position of great difficulty. There was undoubtedly a movement of seditious, if not of revolutionary, tendency at work in the Army. A memorial of a grossly improper character had not only been drawn up, but had been widely circulated among the officers of the Company's service and had received extensive support. Two possible courses were open to the Governor in Council. One was that of conciliation. The Order of the 6th February had evidently been intended as a step in this direction, but in the prevailing temper of the Army it had failed to have any effect. Indeed, so long as the suspension of Major Boles continued, it was hardly to be expected that any measures of conciliation would succeed. This seems to have been to some extent recognized, for attempts were made to induce Major Boles to make some appearance of submission, which would enable the Government to pardon him with a good grace. Major-General Gowdie had himself an interview with Boles and urged him to make some expression of regret, pledging himself that if he did so, he would be restored. Major Boles, however, refused all concession, however formal, and thus made it practically impossible for the Government to retreat from the position which it had taken up.

These overtures towards peaceful settlement of the difficulties with the Army having failed, the only other course open was one of repression. It was hardly possible to ignore the existence of the memorial or the conduct of those who had prepared and circulated it, and the collection of subscriptions for Major Boles was definite evidence of the spirit of insubordination which actuated a large number of the officers. As though to make sure that this was not overlooked, Captain James Grant, who had himself been on Sir George Barlow's staff and who was now with the expeditionary force in Travancore, actually wrote to the Governor's Private Secretary avowing that he had signed the address to Major Boles, and resigning his post as Commandant of the Governor's Bodyguard. Defiance could hardly be more open.

It was now, therefore, determined to take steps to award summary punishment to those officers who were known to be the leaders in the seditious movement. In the month of April Sir George Barlow wrote a minute in which he summed up the information which had been collected, and made proposals as to the action to be taken. The Governor's suggestions were accepted. In an Order dated 1st May, 1809, the penalties decided on were announced. Captain Marshall, Major de Morgan, Captain James Grant and Lieutenant-Colonel St. Leger were suspended from the Service, while Lieutenant-Colonel Chalmers, Colonel Robert Bell, Colonel John Cuppage and Captain Coombs were removed from their staff appointments. The name of Lieutenant-Colonel

Martin was not included as he had already proceeded to England. In referring to Lieutenant-Colonel St. Leger it was remarked that he had taken advantage of the influence derived from the important command entrusted to him by the Government to attempt to subvert the authority of the Governor in Council. Certain minor action was also taken against other officers concerned, including Lieutenant Stock.

While the Government thus dealt with those whom it regarded as the leaders of the seditious movement in the Army, it endeavoured to placate the great body of officers by declarations of confidence. The Governor in Council was convinced, said the Order, that the majority of the Army had resisted the temptation to participate in the dangerous and improper schemes which had necessitated this issue of the Order, and the Government particularly noticed with satisfaction the good conduct of the Hyderabad Subsidiary Force in this respect. A few days later General Gowdie issued, on his own account, a letter to the Army dealing with Major Boles' case. He said that, as the late Commander-in-Chief's farewell manifesto had been clearly illegal on the face of it, Major Boles ought not to have signed it, but that in any case he did not deserve much sympathy, for the Commander-in-Chief had himself tried to induce Major Boles to express regret and had met with a stubborn refusal. He therefore instructed officers in command of Divisions to prevent the circulation of the address to Major Boles or any similar paper.

CHAPTER XIII

EFFECTS ON THE ARMY

The actual effect of the action taken by the Government was very different from what had been expected. When Sir George Barlow issued the Order of the 1st May, 1809, he was undoubtedly under the impression that it would have the effect of finally suppressing the disaffection in the Army. He believed that by removing a few officers who had been the ringleaders in the seditious movement he would re-establish the authority of the Government and restore peace to the distracted military. In a series of letters which he wrote to the Governor-General during the month of April he expresses this view. "I have not a doubt," he wrote on the 16th April, "that we shall go on as smoothly as could be wished in future, the most proper feelings being now very generally entertained with regard to the authority of the Government." [1] On what information this idea was founded cannot now be ascertained, but there is no room for doubt that it was wholly mistaken, as the events which followed proved.

Lieutenant-Colonel St. Leger, after despatching to the Government his letter of the 27th April, set out to return to Trichinopoly. But before he had got

[1] India Office Records: Home, Miscellaneous, Vol. 695.

very far on his way the news of the Government Order of the 1st May reached him, and at Madura he was greeted with further orders prohibiting him from proceeding to Trichinopoly and ordering him to make his way to Poonamallee by way of the east coast. The instructions of the Government added that he should be required to give his word of honour to obey this direction, failing which he should be sent down to Madras under guard.

Meantime the news of the Order of the 1st May had reached the troops in Travancore, and at once produced great excitement. There was little doubt that by now the officers were ripe for mutiny and only needed a leader. An address was at once drawn up and forwarded to Colonel St. Leger at Madura. It declared that the conduct of the Government had been "so oppressive and infamous" that the Army would "rather lose the last drop of their blood than not have redress for the injuries they have already received." It declared that they were all ready to march at a moment's notice and prevent the Order of the 1st May from being carried out, and it appealed to Lieutenant-Colonel St. Leger to lead them. "We sincerely call upon you," said the letter, "as a head, to prevent such infamous proceedings from going forward and we pledge ourselves to die in your cause."

But Lieutenant-Colonel St. Leger was by no means inclined to assume the rôle thus offered him. However ready he was to memorialize and agitate, he had too much sense to approve of mutiny. His belief was in the resources of the law, not in violence. "For

God's sake," he wrote to the authors of the address, "keep quiet and do not have recourse to arms. Keep to firm representations and submission, although against a tyrant." He set an example by obeying the orders of the Government to proceed to Madras by the route indicated, while at the same time he set to work to collect evidence to support his case. He framed an adroit questionnaire, which he sent to the officers who had served under him in Travancore, asking them to say whether he had ever "used any influence as commanding the Travancore Force" to induce them to sign the seditious memorial, and whether he had "attempted the subversion of the authority of the Government of Fort St. George." We know that while in command he had, in fact, asked for signatures to the memorial, but who was to say that in doing so he had "used any influence as commanding the Travancore Force"? Almost all the officers were able conscientiously to answer the Colonel's skilfully framed questions in the negative, and armed with these replies the Colonel felt strong enough to carry the legal war into the enemy's country. Under the advice of lawyers such as Mr. Charles Marsh, soon after he reached Madras, he filed an affidavit in the Supreme Court as a preliminary to an action which he proposed to bring in the Court of King's Bench against Sir George Barlow for unjust suspension and slanderous and malicious libel. He was thus able to leave India with the pleasing consciousness of having made his enemy uncomfortable by the threat of future litigation, and his departure removed the only cool head there was in the military camp.

The G.O. of the 1st May was received in all military stations with the same ebullition of feeling as inspired the address to Colonel St. Leger. The first move was made by the officers of the Hyderabad Subsidiary Force. As soon as the Order reached Secunderabad, the officers determined to make plain to the Governor in Council and to the world at large their scornful repudiation of the Government's words of praise. On the 18th May they circulated a letter addressed to "the officers of the Madras Army," in which, after referring to the "unexpected compliment" offered them in the G.O., they declared that, far from approving of the acts of the Government, they had viewed "with the most lively emotions of concern those extreme acts of power and exertion of authority," and were resolved both to contribute to the support of the suspended officers and to join in "any legal measures of temperance, dignity and firmness" for their restoration. Two days later the officers of the Hyderabad Subsidiary Force on detachment at Jaulna addressed letters of sympathy to Lieutenant-Colonel St. Leger, Lieutenant-Colonel Chalmers, Colonel Bell and Captain Marshall, who were the chief sufferers under the G.O. of 1st May, expressing "surprise and concern" at the treatment those officers had received. To Colonel St. Leger they remarked that the arbitrary manner in which he had been treated "appears to have been adopted for no other reason than that you had nobly exerted yourself to oppose the degradation

. . . of the Service." They also sent messages of support and sympathy to Lieutenant-Colonel Cuppage, Captain Coombs, Captain James Grant and Major de Morgan, and they expressed a wish to contribute to the support of the officers who had suffered for the common cause in which all were united.

Early in June the officers at Secunderabad took a further step. They drew up and despatched an address to Sir George Barlow in which they said that the suspension by Government of so many valuable and respected officers had excited such great and general irritation that they feared the most fatal and disastrous consequences. "Under these impressions we feel compelled to make some effort to avert the evils we see impending or, what may be the possible and probable consequence, the separation of the civil and military authorities." They went on to assure the Government that, with a few exceptions, the whole of the officers of the Madras Army were of but one sentiment and opinion regarding the late acts of Government and considered themselves solemnly pledged to support each other in obtaining redress. While they disclaimed any wish to dictate to the Governor in Council or to comment on his acts, they expressed the opinion that tranquillity would only be restored and the existing ferment removed if the Government Order of the 1st May were rescinded, and if all suspended officers were restored to the Service and to their appointments. This address bore the signatures of 158 officers belonging to the Hyderabad Subsidiary Force.

The receipt of the seditious communications from the officers of the Hyderabad Subsidiary Force and the news of what they were doing had a powerful effect in stirring up the rest of the Army all over the Presidency. It was known that the Subsidiary Force was completely equipped for field service, and its adhesion to the party in favour of revolt was thus an important gain. The movement to raise subscriptions for the suspended officers also spread rapidly. All ranks were eager to contribute. Major Bevan, then a mere boy, mentions in his reminiscences how he had to give up his shooting because he had no money left after subscribing a whole month's pay for the officers "suspended for their opposition to Sir George Barlow." [1]

In every military station Committees were now formed to organize active measures against the Government. Secret communications were sent from station to station. Endless discussions were carried on as to the course to be pursued. Plans were proposed, approved and abandoned. Vows of mutual support were exchanged, but no clear line of policy was agreed on. The wildest rumours were circulated. The Bombay Army had promised, it was said, to support Madras; the Bengal Army was likewise in sympathy. Intense excitement everywhere prevailed. Writing on the 15th June, Lieutenant-Colonel Malcolm said, "It is impossible to convey to men who are calm and think rationally any idea of the state of the Army.

[1] *Thirty Years in India*, 1808–38, by Major H. Bevan, late 27th Regt. M.I., 1839, p. 74.

All respectable men in it appear to suffer a set of mad-headed boys to take the lead; and the greatest merit I see any man claim is that of being passive, though all confess it is a period at which one step will involve the country in all the horrors of a civil war, and there are numbers (such is the insanity that has got head) that desire to accelerate that event." [1]

" There are men now living," wrote Sir John Kaye in 1855, " who look back with astonishment, almost with incredulity, to that period of mutinous excitement. At many of the large Army stations the officers of the Company's regiments avowed themselves ready for any act of daring revolt. They encouraged one another in treason; they talked of fighting against a tyrannical Government in defence of their rights to the last drop of their blood. Seditious toasts were given at the mess-tables and were drunk with uproarious applause. The arrival of every post raised a fever of expectancy. Letters from the disaffected cantonments were eagerly read and instantly circulated. The moral intoxication pervaded all ranks, from the Colonel to the Ensign." If there were any cooler heads among the officers or if any counsels or prudence or sanity were offered, these were swept aside in the flood of excitement.

[1] *Observations on the Disturbances in the Madras Army in* 1809, by Lt.-Col. Malcolm.

CHAPTER XIV

OUTBREAK OF MUTINY AT MASULIPATAM

The first definite act of mutiny was taken at Masulipatam. There were stationed the Company's European Regiment, the first battalion of the 19th Regiment of Native Infantry, a detachment of the 39th Regiment of Native Infantry and a Company of Artillery. The whole force was generally under the command of the officer who commanded the northern division of the Madras Army, but in May 1809 the general officer was absent, and the command of the station fell to the officer in command of the European Regiment.

On the 7th May, 1809, a new commandant arrived. This was Colonel James Innes, a Scotchman from Banff, not perhaps an officer of the highest reputation, for he is referred to in disparaging terms in Captain John Orrok's Letters,[1] and Lieutenant-Colonel William Macleod, writing to Colonel Malcolm,[2] remarks that though Sir George Barlow could have known nothing about Colonel Innes, Sir George's military advisers knew him well, and must have known that he was unfit for the situation. On the day of his arrival, Colonel Innes dined at the Mess of the European Regiment, and a toast was proposed—" The Friends of the

[1] *Letters of John Orrok*, p. 101.

[2] India Office Records : Home, Miscellaneous, Vol. 736.

Madras Army." This does not sound a very outrageous sentiment, but at the time it doubtless had a special significance, and Colonel Innes, who was "a Government man," objected to it, and suggested that it should be altered to "The Madras Army." An altercation arose in which the Colonel received, or imagined that he had received, some affront from some of the younger and more hot-headed officers, and he left the Mess. Next day he called upon Lieutenant Forbes, who had proposed the toast, and Lieutenant Maitland, who was Quartermaster of the regiment, to apologize for their conduct. They refused, and Colonel Innes then reported the matter to Headquarters. He said that his report was merely intended for the private information of the Commander-in-Chief, but nevertheless it was an official report and was treated as such, and a few days later orders were received directing Lieutenant Forbes to proceed to Kondapillai, a small and solitary outpost, and removing Lieutenant Maitland from the post of Quartermaster. These punishments naturally produced a great sensation in the regiment. When Colonel Innes offered the post of Quartermaster to another officer, Lieutenant Spankie, he refused to accept it. Colonel Innes then used words which were interpreted as a reference to the possibility of the regiment's being disbanded. His remark was, of course, repeated, and it added to the alarm and excitement.

By an evil chance an event almost immediately happened which brought the ill-will between the new Colonel and his regiment to a practical issue. Orders had lately arrived from England prohibiting the employment of men belonging to His Majesty's forces as marines on vessels of the Royal Navy. In May 1809 Admiral Drury, who was commanding a squadron on the coast, applied to the Government of Madras for a party of Europeans to serve as marines on board the ships under his command, and the Government issued orders that a detachment should be supplied from the European Regiment at Masulipatam. On 2nd June a further order was received directing Lieutenant Maitland, who had just been removed from the post of Quartermaster, to embark as officer in charge of this detachment and warning Lieutenant Forbes to hold himself in readiness to proceed to Penang, a far-distant and unhealthy settlement.

The receipt of these orders brought to a head the discontent in the regiment. On the 3rd June the officers formed themselves into a Committee, and adopted a resolution to oppose by force the embarkation of the party which was to be sent for service as marines. Although a little later this resolution was rescinded, the excitement was renewed by the arrival of orders for the supply of two more parties of marines. This seemed to lend support to the suspicion that the Government meant to disband the regiment, and the determination to resist was strengthened. When, on the 24th June, the ships which were to embark the men, a frigate and a sloop, appeared in sight, a deputation of officers waited on Colonel Innes and begged him to suspend embarkation until the result of a reference to Government could be known. Colonel

Innes refused. He said that he meant to request the captain of the frigate to land a force to assist him to carry out the embarkation, and that he would also use the detachment of the King's regiment—the 59th Foot —and the Artillery for the same purpose. The deputation retired to the barracks, where the men of the regiment were apparently taken into confidence by their officers.

About one o'clock on the 25th June Colonel Innes gave orders to the Adjutant of the regiment to warn the party told off for service as marines to be ready to embark at 6 p.m. that evening. The news of the issue of this order soon reached the officers and from them was communicated to the men. "Nothing could exceed the tumult which followed in the barracks," says a report; "the men were turned out and their officers were with them." The resolution, which had been adopted three weeks before, to oppose the embarkation of the detachment, was revived, but in order to prevent the risk of a collision between the European Regiment and the King's troops or the sailors, a fresh plan was determined on. About 3 p.m. Major Joseph Storey of the 1st Battalion of the 19th Native Infantry, the officer next in seniority to Colonel Innes, accompanied by a number of other officers, proceeded to the Colonel's bungalow and tried to persuade Colonel Innes to recall his orders and postpone the date of the embarkation. Colonel Innes again refused, and Major Storey then told the Colonel that unless he gave way, he would place him under arrest "for the safety of the garrison." "What?"

cried Colonel Innes. "Place me in arrest, sir? I can place you in arrest and all the officers of the garrison." But in this he was mistaken. Major Storey really held the key to the position, for the men were with him, and he knew it. He therefore told the Colonel that he was under arrest, posted sentries to enforce his orders, and, assuming command of the station, cancelled the instructions for the embarkation of the detachment to serve as marines. Next day he sent to Madras a report of what he had done. At the same time urgent despatches were sent to Secunderabad, to Jaulna, to Seringapatam and to other military stations, telling them what had happened and asking for support. The action of Major Storey at Masulipatam on the 25th June definitely began the mutiny.

The news of what had happened at Masulipatam caused a great increase in the already existing state of excitement. The Committees of officers, which had by now been regularly established in many stations, by mutual communication pledged themselves to support their brother-officers in the Northern Division. It was expected that the Government would immediately resort to force in order to put down the mutiny at Masulipatam, and at Secunderabad, Jaulna and elsewhere, plans were formed to march to the aid of the troops at Masulipatam, should they be assailed.

Although the seriousness of the events in the North was recognized, Sir George Barlow avoided any hasty action. He determined to send up an officer of established reputation and high rank to hold an inquiry and to endeavour to restore discipline. His choice fell on Lieutenant-Colonel John Malcolm, afterwards General Sir John Malcolm and Governor of Bombay. Malcolm had been Private Secretary to Lord Wellesley, in which capacity Sir George Barlow had known him well. Subsequently he had held important political employment both in the Mahratta country and in Persia. He was, therefore, an officer of tried experience, and as he had belonged himself originally to the Madras Army, he must have seemed admirably suited to serve as an envoy from the Government to the recalcitrant garrison at Masulipatam. So indeed he might have been, had he been willing loyally to subordinate his views to those of the Governor and to carry out Sir George Barlow's line of policy.

He reached Masulipatam on the 4th July and at once held a conference with the leading officers. Among them he found an unexpectedly violent feeling prevalent. They were at first inclined to refuse to have anything to do with him, for they had received letters from Secunderabad and Jaulna advising them to regard him as a Government emissary. Though they consented to receive him, they refused altogether to accept his advice. "Speaking under the strong influence of passion," as he says, the officers declared that they had gone too far to retreat. He persuaded them to abandon their plans for an immediate march towards Secunderabad, but further than that they would not go.

On the day of his arrival at Masulipatam, Lieutenant-Colonel Malcolm addressed a letter to Sir George

MAJOR GENERAL SIR JOHN MALCOLM, G.C.B.
From a portrait in the possession of the Oriental Club, London.

Face p. 86.

Barlow in which he painted in the darkest colours the existing position there. Major Storey, he said, was a weak man and the garrison was controlled by a Committee of "violent young men." The delusion that the officers would not proceed to extremities was now completely dissipated, and there was not a single corps within the Presidency that was not committed to resistance to the Government. He considered that the only means of tranquillizing the Army was by the grant of a general amnesty.

Next day, the 5th July, he wrote another and longer letter, in which he repeated his view of the situation and exhorted the Governor to bow before the storm. Not content with mere generalities, he now sent Sir George Barlow a draft of the Government Order which he proposed should be issued. It was long-winded and high-flown in diction, but practically it amounted to nothing less than a complete surrender to the demands of the Army. It spoke of the officers as "a highly meritorious body acting under the strong impulse of warm and honourable but mistaken feelings." It promised to move the Court of Directors to pardon the suspended officers in view of the high character they had held. It restored Colonel Bell to the command of the Artillery at the Mount, Colonel Chalmers to the Travancore Force, and Lieutenant Maitland to the Quartermastership of the European Regiment. It declared a general amnesty for all acts of mutiny or insubordination committed up to that date. The only point not made clear was how Sir George Barlow could continue to be Governor of

Madras after he had thus publicly reversed all his decisions and accepted all the demands of a rebellious soldiery. It has been well said that if anything could have broken down the resolution of Sir George Barlow, it would have been the receipt of such a letter and such proposals from his trusted emissary and representative.

But Lieutenant-Colonel Malcolm was not able to complete his draft without revealing the underlying weakness of the policy which he recommended. This clearly appeared from some of its concluding passages: "The Government," ran the draft, "must declare its positive and final resolution not to alter or modify this proceeding. It will yield no more to the entreaties and demands of the Army; and if any officers are so infatuated and so lost to every consideration of the public good and the general prosperity of the country as not immediately, on the promulgation of this Order, to abandon their present course of proceeding, Government must, however much it may deprecate such an extreme, meet it with that firmness and courage which becomes a constituted authority of the Empire of Great Britain." This passage indicates that Malcolm did not feel certain of the efficacy of his own remedy. The Army, controlled as it was by "violent young men," might not be content with the Government's humiliating concessions and might demand more. In such an event, all that Malcolm could recommend was an exhibition of that "firmness and courage" of which the adoption of his proposals would have proved the absence. The complete bankruptcy of such a course of policy was too obvious for it to run any serious chance of being adopted.

Lieutenant-Colonel Malcolm remained several weeks longer at Masulipatam. The influence which he exerted in keeping the mutinous officers there from worse excesses was undoubtedly valuable. He also wrote several letters from there to friends at Secunderabad and Jaulna which seem to have had a considerable influence.[1] But so far as the mutineers at Masulipatam were concerned, he quite failed to bring them to submit. Probably his sympathy with these misguided men was too strong to enable him, while in actual touch with them, to overcome their prejudices and preconceptions. He seems to have become anxious to escape from his position as soon as possible. He apparently thought that if he returned to Madras, he could persuade the Governor to adopt his views. When, therefore, General Pater arrived and assumed command of the Northern Division, Malcolm left and hurried back to Madras.

On arrival there, however, he found that his influence with the Governor was gone. Sir George Barlow received him civilly, but without cordiality. His trust in Malcolm had obviously been destroyed. As Colonel Close bluntly wrote a few weeks later: "When you departed for Masulipatam, you do not seem to have understood sufficiently the line of proceeding which Sir George Barlow had it in mind to pursue. This I consider as extremely unfortunate."[2] Malcolm had, in fact, intended, not to

[1] See Appendix F, Nos. 6 and 21.

[2] See Appendix F, No. 19.

follow Sir George Barlow's line of policy, but to make Barlow follow his. When he found this was impossible, he threw himself more and more into an attitude of opposition, and became one of Sir George Barlow's most dangerous enemies.[1]

[1] See Appendix E, on Lieutenant-Colonel Malcolm and the Madras Mutiny.

CHAPTER XV

CRITICAL POSITION OF THE GOVERNMENT

COLONEL MALCOLM was by no means alone in urging the Government to surrender to the demands of the Army. Almost every officer in command of a Division—Colonel T. G. Montresor in Secunderabad, Colonel H. Davis in Mysore, Colonel W. Wilkinson in Trichinopoly—sent similar advice, though in less crude terms. Had there been a council of war, it certainly would not have fought on this occasion.

The position indeed became every day more threatening. Not only was Masulipatam in open mutiny, but the Hyderabad Subsidiary Force had also now definitely declared its disobedience to authority. As early as the 5th July the regiments stationed at Jaulna, on the frontiers of Berar, presented their commanding officer with a mutinous address, demanding that no steps should be taken against the mutineers at Masulipatam. At Secunderabad, the headquarters of the Force, when an order arrived directing one of the sepoy regiments, the 2nd battalion of the 10th, to march to Goa, the officers commanding the several regiments in the garrison waited upon Colonel Montresor, who commanded the Cantonment, and requested him to cancel the order to march. He refused, and next day, the 18th July, he was served with a paper signed by Major George Neale of the 1st Regiment of Cavalry and 68 other officers, in which his authority was frankly set at naught and defied. "We," it said, "the officers of the Hyderabad Subsidiary Force, having united in a resolution to obtain redress of grievances, deem any attempt to divide us as incompatible with and destructive of that resolution. We therefore will not consent to the removal of the 2nd Battalion of the 10th Regiment of Native Infantry, whose assistance may soon be necessary to us and whose attachment to our cause we are assured of. But we will nevertheless obey all orders addressed to us by the officer commanding this force for the interior regulation of its duties."

On the 21st July the officers went further. On that date an "ultimatum" addressed to the Government of Madras was presented to Colonel Montresor, which formulated the following specific demands:

1st. The rescindment of the Government Order of the 1st May last, to be acknowledged and published by Government in the same manner as the Order itself.

2nd. The restoration to the Service and to his appointment of every officer who had been removed from any situation or suspended the Service.

3rd. The trial of Lieutenant-Colonel Innes by a General Court-martial for his conduct at Masulipatam while in charge of the Madras European Regiment.

4th. The removal of those officers on the General Staffs who had advised Government to prosecute the measures which had caused the present commotion in the Army.

5th. A general Amnesty to indemnify the proceedings of the Coast Army in the measures they had been forced to adopt.

This "ultimatum" was sent to Lieutenant-Colonel Montresor under a letter signed by six officers commanding regiments who pledged themselves to be satisfied if the Government conceded the above propositions. Lieutenant-Colonel Montresor, in forwarding the papers, assured the Government that the whole of the Army in the Company's service was united in making these demands, and he expressed the opinion that the Government would best consult its dignity by yielding to necessity and thus preventing a sanguinary conflict.

News was soon received of similar occurrences in Travancore. An order had been sent to the force there directing three battalions to march from the headquarters to fresh stations. This order was disobeyed, and the Government's injunctions were defied in the same manner as at Secunderabad. The officers concerned informed Colonel P. Stuart of H.M.'s 19th Regiment, who was in command, that as it was evidently the Government's intention to divide the Native Corps so as to bring them within the power of British regiments, they would not march as directed. Colonel Stuart reported that he was powerless to enforce the orders of the Government. Alarming reports came from all parts of the Presidency, and the expectation of the outbreak of a civil war was widespread.

Fortunately the man who was at the helm in Madras was not easily dismayed. He received unmoved the despairing counsels of Colonel Malcolm and the hesitating advices of his other commanders. Whatever mistakes might hitherto have been laid to Sir George Barlow's account, there is no question but that he faced the alarming situation that now confronted him with extraordinary resolution and courage. There was real danger that a military combination might subvert the civil Government. At the least sign of weakness the regiments would have combined and marched on Madras.

Energetic measures were taken to deal with the crisis. Early in July orders were issued, as already seen, to break up dangerous concentrations of native regiments, and a circular was sent to officers in charge of Divisions calling for a report on the temper of the troops and directing all necessary measures to be taken to maintain discipline. When news came of the critical position in the Hyderabad Subsidiary Force, urgent letters were addressed on the 12th and 14th July to the Governor of Ceylon requesting him to send to Madras all the European Infantry and Cavalry he could spare. On the 14th July Colonel Barry Close, a veteran who had earned renown at the capture of Seringapatam and who commanded great respect among both Europeans and Indians, was instructed to proceed from Poona, where he was Resident, and to assume command at Secunderabad.

A week later, on the 21st July, as the news became generally more threatening, further steps were taken. For the protection of the seat of Government, a camp was formed on the Racecourse at Guindy, and the European troops, as they arrived, were concentrated there. Plans were drawn up for the formation of an Army of 12,000 men, half to be British troops and half trustworthy sepoys. This was placed for the present under the command of Colonel Henry Conran of the 1st Foot. It was proposed that, as soon as it was ready, it should march northward to deal with the threatened trouble in the Hyderabad Subsidiary Force. The Government of Bombay was urgently moved to send whatever British regiments it could spare to assist Madras, and a request was addressed to the Mysore Durbar to supply 2000 Cavalry.

On the 26th July another and still bolder step was taken. The disaffection among the officers of the Madras Army was so widespread, in fact so universal, that their presence with their regiments was everywhere a menace. At any moment they might raise the standard of revolt, and it was decided at once to take steps to separate from their regiments all men who were not prepared at once to bind themselves to obey the orders of Government. Officers in command of divisions and stations were instructed to call on all European officers belonging to the Company's service under their control to sign the following declaration :

> "We, the undersigned officers of the Honourable Company's Service, do, in the most solemn manner, declare upon our word of honour as

> British officers that we will obey the orders and support the authority of the Honourable the Governor in Council of Fort St. George agreeably to the tenor of the Commissions which we hold from the Government."

Any officer refusing to sign this Test was at once to be removed from his military duties and ordered to proceed to the coast, and to reside at any place between Sadras and Negapatam which he might select. Officers thus removed from duty were to be allowed to draw their ordinary pay and allowances while away from their regiments, and were thus offered an inducement to submit quietly to this measure of separation. At the same time the Officers Commanding Divisions were directed to assemble the native officers and to explain to them that some of the European officers, in order to secure advantages for themselves, had disobeyed the orders of Government. It was pointed out that the misconduct of these officers would not benefit the native officers and sepoys, whose duty it was to obey whatever officers the Government might appoint. The Government therefore called on the native officers and sepoys to remain faithful to the Company.

On the 26th and 27th July the orders of Government for the imposition of the Test were successfully carried out in Fort St. George, at the camp near Madras, at St. Thomas' Mount and at Vellore. Although the words of the Test closely followed the terms of the officers' commissions, few consented to sign. Those who did not were removed from duty and their places taken by officers deputed from the King's regiments. Much indignation was expressed at these proceedings. It was said that the officers had been entrapped and taken by surprise. It seems, however, to have been a perfectly legitimate step, having in view the combination against the legal authority of the Government which had admittedly been formed throughout the Presidency.

At other stations the officers in command at first shrank from enforcing the Test, and either made excuses or tried to alter or soften the words prescribed. In every case, prompt orders came from Madras directing the exact execution of the instructions of Government. At Quilon, Colonel Stuart hesitated to call on his officers to sign, representing that they would all refuse. He merely received a curt command to do as he was told. The officers then signed a modified form of Test, promising obedience to all orders provided they were not called on to act against their brother officers. Again the indomitable will in Madras insisted that the prescribed form of Test must be signed without exception or condition. Colonel Stuart was thus compelled to carry out the orders of Government, and all officers but four refused to sign and were suspended. A very similar course of events occurred at Cannanore. Colonel Forbes in command there assured the Government that all was well and strongly deprecated the imposition of the Test. He received stringent orders to carry it out at once. Again a qualified version of the undertaking was tendered, and again it was summarily rejected. At last the orders of the Government were carried out; a few officers signed, but the majority refused and were suspended. The same drama was enacted at other centres—Bellary, Cumbum, Trichinopoly, Dindigul, Madras and Palamcottah. Very few signatures were anywhere obtained. Indeed in the whole Presidency less than 150 officers signed the Test. The rest, to the number of over 1300, including cadets, were removed from their regiments and proceeded to the places indicated for their residence on the east coast.

This separation of the officers from their regiments constituted an important success for the Government. Away from their men the officers were helpless. The regiments thus denuded of their own staffs were provided with fresh commanders from British regiments. The new officers might not know the language of the sepoy, but they could at least be relied upon to obey orders. The regiments, relieved of disaffected officers, instead of being a source of danger to the Government, became an element of strength. The institution of the Test was, in fact, a master stroke of policy. It succeeded through a large area of the Province. At only three centres besides Masulipatam, namely, Secunderabad, Jaulna and Seringapatam, did organized and active resistance afterwards develop.

CHAPTER XVI

THE MUTINY AT SECUNDERABAD

Colonel Close had received the orders of Government directing him to proceed to Secunderabad about the middle of July, but nearly a fortnight passed before he started. He left Poona on the 29th July and proceeded by rapid stages towards Secunderabad. The officers there were by no means inclined to welcome him. A letter was actually sent by the Committee to meet him on his way, telling him that his services were not required and that he was not to come on to Hyderabad, but he took no notice of this prohibition and pushed on as fast as possible towards his destination. He reached Secunderabad on the morning of the 3rd August. Soon after he arrived at the Residency, Colonel Montresor came to see him, and he explained the reason of his coming and the nature of his orders, which left him no option but to assert the authority with which he was invested. They went together towards the Cantonment, sending word to the officers to meet him there. No attempt was made to prevent his entering, and the main picket turned out under arms and saluted, but none of the officers to whom he sent summonses appeared. Major Neale, the senior officer of the Company's troops, and Major Deacon were, however, present, and Colonel Close read to them the text of the Test and impressed upon them that they should either sign it or withdraw from all exercise of military function. Major Neale, who had seemed "strongly affected" at meeting the Colonel, replied that the Government's terms did not offer any security for their brother officers at Masulipatam. He urged that the officers were firmly united by ties and that they could not now withdraw without redress, and he asked for time to consult the other officers. Colonel Close, however, pressed him to decide at once, reminding him of his long service and his rank, and urging him to take this chance of an honourable retreat. The Major was deeply affected by this appeal, but said it was impossible for him to accept either of the alternatives offered to him by the Government.

The appeal to the European officers having thus failed, Colonel Close said that he now felt himself at liberty to take another course and to communicate direct with the native soldiery. Turning to a troop of cavalry, which was drawn up near, he explained to them that a dispute had arisen between the officers and the Government, and pointed out that this did not affect the native troops, whose allegiance was to the Government. The men seemed to listen and to assent to what he said, but at that moment he saw the sepoys of the 2nd battalion of the 16th Regiment rushing out of their place of arms and forming in divisions immediately in front of him. The British officers were exerting themselves to form the divisions with regularity. Colonel Close rode into the divisions, calling on the native officers to let him know why they had taken to their arms, and urging them to obey him as the representative of the Government. He appealed particularly to one native officer, taking him by the shoulder and asking him why the men were priming and loading, but he could get no reply. He advanced to the front division of the battalion, but could get no one to listen to him. By this time four battalions were formed up with artillery in the middle, and there is some reason to think that it was intended to seize the person of Colonel Close. If so, he met the crisis with great adroitness. When Major Neale and Major Deacon approached and expressed their deep regret that any circumstances should place them in opposition to the Colonel, Close replied that he should consider Major Neale particularly responsible for what had occurred; that as the object of his visit had been defeated, he should consider himself as Major Neale's prisoner; and that Colonel Montresor should be regarded as still commandant. He then accompanied Colonel Montresor to his quarters. A little later all the Field Officers came to see him and begged him to proceed to Madras to exercise his influence there on behalf of the Army, but Colonel Close, unlike Colonel Malcolm at Masulipatam, altogether declined to undertake any such mission or to receive any address or personal application. Next day he received a letter from the Committee of officers requesting him to leave the place in the course of the day, "lest more unpleasant decisive measures should be necessary." Colonel Close accordingly left

Hyderabad, with the intention of retiring gradually towards Poona and awaiting further instructions from the Government.

Colonel Close's courageous attempt to bring the officers to reason thus ended in apparent failure. He seems to have confronted a very difficult position with great ability and to have been in considerable personal danger, as at one time some of the younger men wanted to open fire on him.[1] The sepoy regiments were in a state of great unrest, and on the night of the 4th, on some trifling alarm, the whole line turned out and three of the corps beat to arms, being apprehensive of an attack by the 33rd King's Regiment. Urgent messages were sent to Jaulna and to Masulipatam, calling on the troops at those stations to join them. It seems also to have been in contemplation to move from Secunderabad and advance towards Madras. On the 8th August the "Select Committee" sent to Colonel Montresor a notice that they proposed to separate themselves from his command, to camp close to the Cantonment, and to adopt regulations with which he could not be allowed to interfere.

But a dramatic change in the position was now at hand. Colonel Close's appearance, his exhortations to the officers and the revulsion of feeling caused by seeing the veteran commander treated with contumely had not been without effect both on the officers and the sepoys. A letter had also been received from Colonel Malcolm at Masulipatam, laying clearly before the officers the consequences of persistence in their mutinous opposition to the Government, and this

[1] See Appendix F, Letter No. 15.

seems to have had considerable influence.[1] Moreover, doubts as to the eventual attitude of the native troops were beginning to be felt. When, on the 9th August, Colonel Montresor received the Committee's letter of the 8th, he addressed a moving appeal to Major Neale, as the senior of the revolting officers, entreating him and his companions to reflect upon the consequences of their conduct, and pointing out the dangers which they were about to encounter and the guilt they would incur. He exhorted the senior officers to advise the juniors of the ruin that awaited them, and he begged them not to be deluded by their passions and a false point of honour. Apparently on the same day, the 9th August, he also had an interview with the leaders, and to calm their minds he gave them a promise that he would not use His Majesty's 33rd Regiment against them unless they first resorted to violence. The combined effect of these exhortations and of the information coming in regarding the determined attitude of the Government turned the scale. On the 9th August Major Neale wrote to Lieutenant-Colonel Montresor withdrawing their notice of the previous day, and asking him to "favour them by taking steps" to remove any unfavourable impression it might have produced at Madras. On the 11th August, an address was drawn up to the Governor-General declaring their loyalty, explaining that their refusal to submit to Colonel Close was because of "the sudden and unexpected manner" in which he presented them the Test, throwing themselves on the justice, clemency and wisdom of the Governor-General, and begging

[1] See Appendix F, Letter No. 6.

for a general amnesty to themselves and all those who had engaged in "the late unhappy events." This was signed by all the officers in the garrison, who at the same time also signed the Test, which had been prescribed on the 26th July, and thus completed their submission to the Government. The officers also wrote to those at Jaulna, Masulipatam, Gooty and Seringapatam, sending a copy of the address to Lord Minto, with the following addition: "The above address, with the Test, has been signed by all the officers of this Force. Imperious circumstances demanded and mature reflection compelled them to this measure, which they earnestly implore their brother officers to adopt as speedily as possible."

By these proceedings the mutiny at Secunderabad, which was much the most dangerous of the storm-centres in the Madras Army, was practically brought to an end. The Government of Madras, to whom the news must have indeed been welcome, expressed their "high gratification" at the return of the officers to a sense of duty. The Nizam, who had been considerably alarmed at the rumours flying about, was greatly reassured by the intelligence conveyed to him by the Resident, Captain Thomas Sydenham. Colonel Close, waiting anxiously somewhere on the road to Poona for further news and orders, must have been greatly gratified. Only in the ranks of the mutinous officers was the step taken at Secunderabad received with expressions of rage and disgust, for there could be no mistaking the fact that this surrender portended the breakdown of the entire revolt.

CHAPTER XVII

THE MUTINY AT JAULNA

While these events had been proceeding at Secunderabad, the mutiny had followed a different course at Jaulna. Jaulna was a frontier cantonment where was assembled a detachment of the Hyderabad Subsidiary Force, consisting of two regiments of Native Cavalry, three battalions of Native Infantry, a squadron of Horse Artillery and a proportion of Company's Artillery. This force was collected to guard the frontier of our ally, the Nizam of Hyderabad. At the moment, a large body of Mahratta horse under Meer Khan, whom Colonel Close described as the first native military leader in India, was threatening an attack, and the Mahratta forces were an ever-present danger. But, as in Bengal in 1766, the presence of an enemy had no effect in turning the officers of the Army from their mutinous intentions. The Jaulna force was under the command of Lieutenant-Colonel John Doveton of the 8th Regiment of Native Cavalry.

The news of the mutiny at Masulipatam reached Jaulna at the beginning of July, and on the 5th of that month the officers commanding the corps and detachments of the Berar Force waited on Colonel Doveton with an address to the Governor-General, the object of which was to acquaint Lord Minto with their feelings on hearing of the mutiny at Masulipatam, and to warn him of the consequences which would ensue if severe measures were taken against the mutinous officers. Colonel Doveton at once forwarded the address to the Commander-in-Chief, to the Officer Commanding at Secunderabad and to Captain Thomas Sydenham, Resident at Hyderabad. Next day, in a private letter to Captain Sydenham, he wrote in hysterical terms of the position at Jaulna: "Horror on horror! My dear Sydenham, since I sent off my express to you of this date, circumstances have been made known to me that make my blood run cold. . . . I (have) learnt with astonishment from a deputation of (officers) that they, as well as the Subsidiary Force at Secunderabad, have actually pledged themselves in the most solemn manner to support the Northern Division of the Army and to march to their assistance, should Government make use of coercive measures against them. This, you see, leaves no option. I must either arrest the whole of the officers of the detachment or must suffer myself to be deposed from my position. The first presents immediately to the mind the horrid, horrid picture of a general massacre of the whole by the native part of the detachment, and the latter one little better. What is to be done in this dreadful extremity?"

In reply Captain Sydenham sent a reassuring letter. He pointed out that there was no reason to suppose that the Government meant to use force against the mutinous officers at Masulipatam. Colonel Malcolm had been sent there to hold an inquiry, and had arrived and quietly assumed command. He therefore advised Colonel Doveton to point out to the officers that they were the advanced post of the Army, situated in foreign territory, surrounded by enemies to the British cause, and to urge on them the terrible consequences that might follow if they abandoned their duty. He exhorted Colonel Doveton to use his influence to get the officers to withdraw their address, which had evidently been written on the first impulse after the news from Masulipatam was received, and to keep quiet.

This advice was not without effect, and no further steps towards a mutiny were taken at Jaulna for some time. On the 23rd July the officers even consented to withdraw their address to the Governor-General, though more because it was no longer appropriate to changed circumstances than from any change of sentiment. By that time the officers had appointed a Committee, which now began to speak as representing the force, and which, as Colonel Doveton said, although illegal, "possessed the confidence and represented the general sentiments of all the officers under his command except his personal staff." The attitude of this Committee fluctuated with the news that was received from other stations. At one moment the more extreme opinions, which advocated an immediate march to join the other disaffected corps, prevailed, and at other times more moderate or more timid counsels gained the ascendancy. On the 25th July a resolution was forwarded by the Committee to Colonel Doveton in the following terms:—

"Having united among ourselves and also united with the whole Army in a resolution to obtain redress of our grievances, the particulars of which have already been laid before Government, we deem any attempt to divide us as incompatible with and destructive to that resolution. We shall therefore disregard any order to that effect. But we will nevertheless obey all orders addressed to us by the officer commanding this force for the internal regulation of its duty." In sending him this resolution, the Committee declared that it did so "with infinite pain," and declared that no disrespect was intended towards the Colonel, whom they assured of their "unalterable esteem." On his side Colonel Doveton, addressing his letter to "The Officers styling themselves the Jaulna Committee," acknowledged the receipt of the resolution and announced that he had forwarded it to the Officer Commanding at Hyderabad and to the Resident there.

Colonel Doveton was in a difficult position. His sympathies were, beyond doubt, with the officers, belonging, as they did, to the same service as himself. But he had not quite forgotten his duty to the Government, and he seems to have striven for a considerable time to keep the mutinous element from any step from which there was no retreat. In particular, he used his influence to prevent the force from leaving Jaulna. In order to do that, he seems to have gone great lengths, promising the officers that in certain eventualities he would put himself at their head. As late as the 9th August he wrote to the Resident at Hyderabad that another "peremptory call" had come from the Committee at Secunderabad, but that, in consequence of his opposition, he believed the officers had again given up the idea of moving. By thus delaying the march of the detachment from Jaulna, Lieutenant-Colonel Doveton undoubtedly did good service to the cause of law and order.

But either his power, or his will, to restrain the officers was gradually exhausted. One of the intercepted letters [1] gives a clear account of how Colonel Doveton finally gave way. Apparently the news of the removal of the officers from their regiments at Madras and St. Thomas' Mount gave the finishing touch. On the 12th August he determined to throw in his lot with the mutiny. He agreed to lead the troops south, and he addressed the sepoys in the vernacular at a parade on the evening of that day and explained his intentions. Next day the orders for the march were issued. At the same time a "Declaration" was drawn up. This was addressed "To all Officers, Civil or Military, both of His Majesty's and the Honourable Company's service, to the Troops, both European and Native, and to the Inhabitants of the countries under the Government of the Presidency of Fort St. George." It said that the officers of the Jaulna Force, being on the eve of commencing their march, felt bound "solemnly and publicly to avow the cause and motives of their proceeding." It went on to declare that they had learnt that the Madras Government were intending to proceed to extremities

[1] See Appendix F, Letter No. 16.

against the officers and troops of the Company. "We march," said the Declaration, "to prevent the wanton effusion of human blood; to prevent the arraying of one portion of the Army in battle against the other; to prevent the dreadful consequences to our Country, as well as to the officers and troops themselves, which must ensue from the lamentable obstinacy of the Honourable the Governor in Council." It went on to declare that they marched to obtain from the Governor in Council an assurance to abstain from acts of unnecessary severity until the Court of Directors could deal with their grievances, and also to obtain the Governor in Council's assent to a general amnesty and to the restoration to the Service of all officers, both civil and military, who, "under the present grievous system," had been suspended. It was added that they were solemnly sworn to persevere till death in the above determination. To this document Lieutenant-Colonel Doveton affixed his signature, and it bears internal evidence of being his composition.

On the 14th August the march actually began. A Havildar's guard was left from each battalion to protect the houses of the officers and sepoys until the return of the detachment. Colonel Doveton marched with the troops, who advanced eight miles on the 14th, and on the 15th a light detachment, consisting of the Horse Artillery and flank companies, was directed to be prepared to move in advance of the rest of the column and to make rapid marches towards Hyderabad. It actually reached Purtoor, thirty miles from Jaulna, when news was received of the submission of the officers at Secunderabad. This was a terrible blow to Lieutenant-Colonel Doveton. At first he intended to proceed, but after a night's reflection he changed his mind. On the 16th August he announced to the troops that it would be leading them to certain destruction to go on and that they must return to Jaulna. No opposition was offered, and the force began to retrace its steps. It reached Jaulna again on the 18th August, and its return was duly reported to the Resident at Hyderabad, and to the officer commanding at Secunderabad.

To the officers of the Jaulna Force this return was a bitter mortification. In a letter addressed from Jaulna on the day of their return to the officers at Masulipatam they said: "The whole of the Jaulna Force marched on the 14th and advanced to Puttoor, thirty miles distant, when we were made acquainted with the defection of the officers at Secunderabad, who, to their eternal disgrace, have signed an unconditional submission. Comments on so foul an act are unnecessary. The consequence has been the return of the troops to Jaulna, where we are, to a man, resolved either to obtain honourable terms or perish nobly in a cause which must have succeeded but for the dastardly conduct of a few who, to save themselves, have sacrificed those whom they were solemnly and sacredly pledged to support." Similar sentiments are expressed in other intercepted letters,[1] and it is possible to estimate from these expressions how valuable a service to the cause of peace Lieutenant-Colonel Doveton had performed in so long deferring the march of the detachment.

[1] See Appendix F, Letter No. 21.

On the 26th August Lieutenant-Colonel Doveton thought it necessary to offer to the Government of Madras, through the Resident in Hyderabad, an explanation of the part which he had played in this affair. The events at Madras and Secunderabad had, he said, so inflamed the minds of the officers that, if he had not consented to march, they would have marched without him. He therefore thought it better to put himself at their head in order that he might perhaps be able to prevent bloodshed. He did not explain, however, how this reason applied to his conduct in haranguing the native officers on the 12th August and inducing them to make a movement which was intended to end in the subversion of the civil government.

On 4th September the officers themselves sent in their submission. With almost cynical effrontery, they observed that "they would do injustice to the patriotism and loyalty which had always actuated their conduct if they were to hesitate in affording to the Government an unequivocal and satisfactory proof of their sentiments on the present occasion." They referred to the choice which the Government offered to the Army between signing the Test and quitting their regiments. They felt, they said, that they could not withdraw from their regiments "without exposing the national interests to imminent risks." It was true that they had made a "short movement" towards Hyderabad, but they had soon returned. No harm had been done, and they trusted that that little error would be condoned. They had now signed the Test, and they hoped that this "spontaneous act" would convince the Government of their determination to support its authority. They had also written a letter to the officers in Seringapatam, adjuring them to follow their example. The contrast between these sentiments and those expressed only a fortnight before in the letter of the 18th August is significant. It was now the turn of the Jaulna officers to advise submission and to break the sacred pledges by which they had sworn to shed "the last drop of their blood." But by this time the cry "Sauve qui peut" was becoming general.

Lieutenant-Colonel Doveton in forwarding to Captain Sydenham the submission of the officers expressed his own feelings on the subject. "Nothing remains," he wrote, "but to congratulate ourselves on the favourable termination of the late dreadful disputes, and I can most truly assure you that no man on earth can be more grateful to Divine Providence on this head than I am." In this pious reflection we may doubtless recognize a touch of genuine sentiment. The worthy Colonel was not born to ride the whirlwind and direct the storm.

CHAPTER XVIII

THE MUTINY IN THE NORTH

LIEUTENANT-COLONEL MALCOLM, as has been seen, left Masulipatam on the 22nd July. Although in his own account of the transactions he carefully avoids mention of any understanding with the mutinous officers there, it seems extremely probable that when he left he gave the officers hopes of a favourable settlement. The advice which he gave to Sir George Barlow suggests such a conclusion, and the lull which occurred at Masulipatam for ten days after he left supports it. On the 2nd August we find General Pater sending a report of an interview which he had had with the mutineers in which he expressly says that their agitation was increased owing to their not having received any news from Colonel Malcolm. On this date the officers sent notice to Captain Morehouse, whose fidelity to their cause was doubtful, to leave the Fort. Next day, the 3rd August, General Pater reports the issue by the Officers' Committee of a Garrison order directing the European Regiment, the 1st Battalion 19th Native Infantry and the Artillery to be ready for immediate field service, and ordering the submission at once of indents for such camp equipage as would be required. Similar reports of preparations for a march were sent in on the 5th and 6th August, but it is not certain whether the Masulipatam garrison contemplated junction with the Hyderabad Subsidiary Force or an advance on Madras. A little later the Assistant Magistrate at Masulipatam told the Government that the troops were in perfect readiness, and would have marched on the 8th August, but that on that day Calcutta newspapers arrived containing Lord Minto's order of the 21st July, and this had led to postponement.

Although the decision to march was deferred, the officers at Masulipatam soon found themselves forced to take various violent and illegal actions. Money was needed to pay the troops, and the treasury officer was forced to issue supplies of coin. Correspondence arriving by post was seized, and on the 12th August it is reported that Colonel Innes had been ordered to leave the Fort. Mention is made of some of the men of the European Regiment being drunk and threatening to loot. News now came of the surrender of the officers at Secunderabad, but this termination to the revolt was by no means at first acquiesced in at Masulipatam. On the 15th, General Pater, having ordered a parade of the troops in garrison, entered the Fort and read to them a declaration from the Government promising pardon to the rank and file if they submitted. The officers allowed him to make this announcement without interruption, and indeed encouraged him to do so. But when he had finished and called on those men who accepted the offers of Government to step forward, not a man moved, and the troops marched off with shouts of "Our officers," "Grievances," "Bengal Allowances," "The last drop of blood for our officers," etc. It was clear that the soldiers, European and Indian alike, were not at all ready to abandon the cause for which the mutiny had been begun.

The first actual movement towards surrender came from the officers. They were better informed as to the true state of affairs, and the impossible position in which they were placed became daily clearer.

On the 16th August, Major Storey and Captain Andrews, the leaders of the mutiny, addressed a letter to the General in which they admitted that the time had now arrived when they found they could no longer oppose the measures of the Government of Madras without injury to the interests of their country. "It is true," they said, "that we have been driven to the brink of insurrection," but they were now prepared to submit. When, however, General Pater on the 17th entered the Fort to take charge of the garrison, a serious situation arose. The rank and file of the European Regiment began to be suspicious that they were being betrayed. They did not understand the sudden change of front which had occurred in the last few days. No clear account exists of what happened, but General Pater reported that he had been placed in so critical a position that a general massacre would have occurred if he had not promised a pardon to both officers and men without distinction. As he had hinted only the day before that he intended to exercise his discretion in dealing with the expected surrender, it is not impossible that his account gives rather an exaggerated view of the trouble. At any rate the officers submitted and signed the Test.

But the dangers inherent in such a mutiny were not yet at an end. On the 20th August serious disturbances broke out at Masulipatam. An artillery soldier struck a sepoy near Major Storey's house and in his presence. Major Storey remonstrated with the artillery man, who replied that he should do as he liked. Angered by this insolent reply, Major Storey seems to have tried to horsewhip the artillery man, whereupon the latter made off to his barracks and returned with some 200 soldiers of the Artillery Corps armed with loaded guns and threatening to kill Major Storey. The Major had to fly on a bare-backed horse, and reaching the Fort collected a force of 200 sepoys, but meantime General Pater and other officers had pacified the Artillery, and Major Storey was able to return to his house, though he thought it safer to keep a guard for his protection. On the 3rd September, orders arrived from the Government declining to confirm the general pardon granted by General Pater, and ordering that the European Regiment and the 19th Native Infantry should be sent down to Madras. This marked the end of the mutiny.

The evil example set by the officers at Masulipatam had been widely imitated in the Northern Command, and acts of mutiny had been committed at many stations. On the 6th August, the 1st Battalion of the 24th Regiment stationed at Ellore arrested their commanding officer, Lieutenant-Colonel Fletcher, and prevented him from holding any communication with the General at Masulipatam. On the 12th August, officers and men of the 1st Battalion of the 11th Regiment of Native Infantry seized the Government treasure at Cocanada. A few days later the Judge at Rajahmundry reported that the same regiment had also seized the Treasury at Rajahmundry, had taken possession of the Post Office, had seized all boats on the river, and had prohibited the publication of any orders which the Government might issue. Almost at the same time the Collector of Vizagapatam announced that the officers belonging to the detachment of the 1st Battalion of the 21st Regiment N.I. had seized the Treasury there and carried off 550,000 rupees. Fortunately these things happened too late to affect the general fortunes of the movement. In a few days the officers who had thus misbehaved saw the necessity of retracing their steps. Those at Ellore signed the Test on the 20th August. On the 23rd the officers of the 11th Regiment promised to restore the treasure seized at Cocanada and to return to their duty at Samulkota. On the 30th August the treasure taken possession of at Vizagapatam was also replaced, and before the end of the month all the mutinous officers in the Northern Command had submitted and signed the Test.

CHAPTER XIX

THE MUTINY AT SERINGAPATAM

At Masulipatam, Secunderabad and Jaulna the mutiny of officers was brought to a conclusion without bloodshed or loss of life. Unhappily at Seringapatam the result was different.

The garrison of the Fort of Seringapatam consisted of the 2nd Battalion of the 15th Regiment of Madras Infantry, commanded by Lieutenant-Colonel Robert Munro, the 2nd Battalion of the 19th Regiment of Madras Infantry, commanded by Major D. C. Kenny, 120 men of the King's 80th Regiment, and 300 European Artillerymen. The Commandant of the Fort was Lieutenant-Colonel John Bell of the Madras Artillery, who had been on leave out of India in 1808 and only returned to Madras in February 1809. He could therefore claim to have been unprejudiced by any of the events during Lieutenant-General Macdowall's tenure of office, and to have come back with an open mind on the subject of the officers' discontent. When, early in July, Sir George Barlow called for a report on the state of feeling of the troops, and Lieutenant-Colonel Davis, commanding in Mysore, made a reference both to Colonel Bell and to Lieutenant-Colonel Munro of the 15th, both officers assured him that no act of violence or hostile movement was contemplated, though they admitted that there was but one sentiment throughout the Army, and that a regular system of communication had been established between all the stations of the coast troops, and even with some in Poona and Bengal. A few days later, however, on 26th July, a much more alarming account of the position was sent to the Government by Mr. A. H. Cole, in charge of the Mysore Residency. He said that dissatisfaction was general among the Company's officers throughout Mysore, and that he was certain that there was no extremity whatever to which they would not proceed in order to attain their ends. The slightest indication of the Government's intention to put down this movement by force would, he knew, close the gates of Seringapatam against their orders, and he did not believe that there was a single garrison or outpost of Company's troops in Mysore which was not prepared at a moment's notice to march to the assistance of Seringapatam.

Meantime orders had been issued by the Government directing the 2nd Battalion of the 19th Native Infantry and the Company of Artillery to move from Seringapatam to Bangalore, where there were two British regiments and where, therefore, the Company's troops would be under more control. But as soon as these orders were known, the officers at Seringapatam showed signs of an intention to resist. Addresses were drawn up by the officers of all three Corps—2nd 15th, 2nd 19th and Artillery—saying they heard it was the intention of Sir George Barlow to separate the Company's troops and to seize their officers. They referred to the collection of troops near Madras and to the reinforcements from Ceylon and Bombay, and they claimed the protection of their commanding officers. Colonel Bell, in forwarding these addresses, said that an attempt to enforce the order of transfer would provoke an outbreak such as had happened at Masulipatam, and asked that the transfer might be deferred "until the cause of alarm is done away." This incident, if it did not amount to actual mutiny, showed the insubordinate condition of the garrison and confirmed Mr. Coles' report.

On the 29th July, the Government's order of the 26th regarding the Test having been received, Lieutenant-Colonel Davis proceeded to Seringapatam to carry out its instructions. He found the Fort in a state of great excitement. A report had been spread that the Government meant to surprise the place, and the sepoys had manned the walls, while the Artillery, with a number of guns, had taken possession of the gates. Lieutenant-Colonel Davis was allowed, however, to enter, and as it was late he took no action that night. Next morning he wrote to Colonel Bell, directing him to instruct the officers of the garrison to come and see him at 10 a.m.

Up to noon no one appeared, but at that hour Colonel Munro, accompanied by a number of officers, but without Colonel Bell, arrived. Their first inquiry was whether Lieutenant-Colonel Davis had received instructions to secure their persons and to separate them by force from their regiments. On this point he was able to give them assurances, and he read to them the Test as it had been laid down by the Government, and asked them to sign it. To this, however, there was no response, and Colonel Munro asked to be allowed to take away the formula for consideration. This was agreed to and the officers withdrew.

After some time information was brought to Lieutenant-Colonel Davis that no one was allowed to leave the Fort without an order from Colonel Bell, and he then wrote to Colonel Bell, saying that he intended to return to Mysore that afternoon, and requesting that orders should be issued to allow him and his staff to pass. For some hours no answer was returned, but at 5 p.m. Lieutenant-Colonel Munro brought a message, which was said to emanate from Colonel Bell, to the effect that Lieutenant-Colonel Davis might save himself the trouble of getting into his palanquin as he would not be permitted to pass the gates. News also came that Mr. Smith, the Paymaster, had actually been stopped and turned back. It looked, therefore, as though the officers intended to hold Lieutenant-Colonel Davis a prisoner, but if this was ever thought of, the design was soon abandoned. After an interval of an hour and a half, a deputation from the "Committee of Officers" arrived, and assured Colonel Davis that there had never been any intention of putting any restraint on his person or on that of his staff, and that the guard that had been placed over his house was a guard of honour. On this announcement Lieutenant-Colonel Davis at once left the Fort and returned to Mysore. Throughout this day—the 29th July—the drawbridges of the Fort had been up and the garrison under arms, and Colonel Bell had issued orders that fire was to be opened on any armed body of men coming along the Bangalore or Mysore roads or crossing the bridge.

The same day in the morning Mr. James Casamajor, Acting Judge and Magistrate in Seringapatam, determined to send the Government treasure from the Fort to Mysore, but the sepoys at the gates refused to let it pass without an order from Colonel Bell. Mr. Casamajor accordingly wrote to Colonel Bell, but he was told in reply that the removal of the treasure would cause alarm among the inhabitants and that it should stay where it was. Next morning, the 30th July, a party of sepoys under the command of Captain John Turner of the 15th Regiment Native Infantry came to the cutcheri and took possession of the Treasury and its contents, which included about 11,000 pagodas, though he refused to sign a receipt for it. Mr. Casamajor went to see Colonel Bell, who, however, refused to see him. He then reported the seizure by letter to Colonel Bell, but was told that the Colonel had resigned the command of the Fort to a Committee of Officers and therefore could not receive his letter. Mr. Casamajor thereupon left the Fort and proceeded to Mysore, whence he despatched a report to Government. Next day, 31st July, Mr. Smith, the Paymaster, who had remained in Seringapatam, received a letter from Captain George Cadell, the Town Major, telling him that Colonel Bell had deemed it advisable to put a guard over the

Treasury and not to allow it to be opened without his orders. From that time onwards the mutinous officers were entirely in control of the Treasury and made such disbursements from it as they chose. The public granaries were also taken possession of and grain issued as required.

A large consignment of treasure, some 30,000 pagodas, was at this moment on its way from the Ceded Districts to Seringapatam. When this consignment was approaching its destination it was met by two messengers sent by Colonel Davis, who told the escort to proceed by a circuitous route to Mysore. As these messengers had no written order, the Havildar in charge of the escort halted and sent a naick and sepoy to the Fort to seek instructions. About midnight a detachment of sepoys came from the Fort, took charge of the treasure, and took it into Seringapatam, where it was held by the insurgent officers. This seizure of the consignment seems to have occurred on the night of the 1st–2nd August, and on the 2nd August a strong party of sepoys, with guns, was sent from the Fort into the Mysore country with the object apparently of clearing away any hostile Mysore troops.

On the 3rd August an attempt was made by the responsible authorities to bring the mutinous officers to reason. A letter signed both by Colonel Davis and by Mr. A. H. Cole was addressed to "Colonel Bell and the officers in control of the Fort of Seringapatam," exhorting them to submit to the orders of Government, and promising to overlook the personal indignities that had been offered to them and to do their best to get the officers exonerated if, even at that late moment, they would sign the Test. No reply was apparently made, but on the same day Colonel Bell transmitted to Colonel Davis declarations signed by the officers of the several Corps in Seringapatam, intimating that the moment the grievances were redressed, they would sign the Test, but that "as the intention at present of that obligation is evidently to bind ourselves down to shed the blood of our own brother soldiers, we must decline affixing our names thereto." In sending in these papers Colonel Bell also transmitted the Test, which he had himself signed, and added, "I shall remain here while there is hope left of doing well, unless I receive orders from you to the contrary." This seems to have been merely a subterfuge intended either to throw dust in the eyes of the Officer Commanding or to serve as a bridge of escape should Bell afterwards be called to account for his actions. On receipt of this letter, Lieutenant-Colonel Davis at once replied in friendly, almost affectionate terms, saying:

> "I thank you for your communications, my heart and house, and those of Mr. Cole, are open to you; and whatever arrangement can convenience you will be readily agreed to."

To this appeal Colonel Bell made no response.

Up to this time the small detachment of His Majesty's 80th Regiment had remained in the Fort of Seringapatam, although, since Colonel Bell had ordered the sentries to fire on any Mysore troops that might pass the bridge, the officer in command of the detachment had not allowed them to mount guard. But their presence was evidently regarded as a constraint, and perhaps as a source of danger to the mutineers, and on the 3rd August, Colonel Bell ordered the detachment to leave the Fort and march to Bangalore. He advised Lieutenant Adamson, who was in command, not to go near Mysore, as he might depend upon it that "Mysore would be in ashes in a few days." These words lent colour to the rumours which were in existence at the time, that the revolting garrison was considering the question of attacking Mysore. Lieutenant-Colonel Davis, writing on the 4th August to the Chief Secretary to Government, said: "Seringapatam is strong, desperate and well furnished with a fine park of European artillery, and reports have more than once come to our knowledge that it was their intention to make a night attack upon the weak and defenceless fort of Mysore, though it is as well secured as any common country work will admit." On the 5th August, however, Colonel Bell wrote that "the Board of Officers who control this garrison have come to the determination not to be the first aggressors in the present alarming crisis."

While the mutinous officers hesitated, the Government continued their preparations. Orders were sent to Colonel Gibbs at Bangalore to enforce the Test in the regiments composing the garrison, and after some demur this was done. The result was that all the officers refused to sign. But they offered no resistance to the order of suspension, and they were accordingly removed from their regiments and sent to Hoosoor, officers from the King's regiments taking their place. The result was as the Government had foreseen. The sepoys, separated from their disaffected officers, were no longer dangerous. It became possible, therefore, for Colonel Gibbs to advance with the British troops towards Seringapatam, thus relieving Mysore from any danger of being attacked by the mutinous forces.

On the 6th August, Colonel Bell, in spite of his having signed the Test and of his declaration that he was no longer in command of Seringapatam, took a curious step. He addressed a letter to Purniah, the Diwan of Mysore, complaining that the Diwan had "without the authority and consent of the Supreme Government" broken one of the principal articles of the treaty between Mysore and the Company, and had committed other acts hostile to their interests by stopping supplies to the British garrison in Seringapatam. "If," said Colonel Bell, "these acts of aggression are not immediately repealed, I shall consider open hostilities to have been commenced by the Mysore Government against the Honourable Company Bahadur." To this the Diwan replied that all that had been done had been done by the order of the Resident in Mysore, who had been appointed by the Governor-General. Colonel Bell did not, however, abandon his somewhat childish attempt to pretend that he and his mutinous garrison represented the Government of India, for he sent Purniah a second letter on the 9th August, saying that he found that "in spite of treaties, good faith and the sight of God," the Diwan had caused British officers and native troops crossing the Mysore State to be seized. Therefore he felt himself in honour bound to seize "on all your people in the Fort" and to detain all property in the Fort belonging to the Raja or the Diwan. Purniah replied, with some humour, that he had "never before seen two authorities of the British Government," and that he recognized only the accredited officers of the Governor-General, *i.e.* Colonel Davis and Mr. Cole.

In pursuit of the same pretence that he was acting on behalf of the Governor-General, Colonel Bell addressed a letter on the 9th August to Lord Minto. He said that he had used "every endeavour to obtain Colonel Davis' confidence and that of Mr. Cole in order to learn what are the real intentions of the Government in regard to this place." Having failed in this endeavour, he now addressed the Governor-General direct in order to solicit his instructions "on the line of conduct I am to pursue in this difficult pass." In a postscript he added that he learnt that an encampment had been formed about 2½ miles from the Fort, presumably by the European force from Bangalore, and he added: "Everything here is in readiness for the defence I am determined to make until I receive your Excellency's instructions." At the same time he wrote to Colonel Davis, that, to guard against the Fort being surprised, he intended to cut the abutments of the bridge, which would probably result in its being washed away by the river, unless Colonel Davis, Mr. Cole and the Diwan of Mysore would promise that no attempt should be made to occupy the island or to prevent the detachments in Mysore from joining him if they wished to do so.

News had already been received that the detachments of the 8th and 15th Native Infantry at Chittledrug, numbering about 1120 officers and men, under pressing invitations from Colonel Bell, had left their station and were advancing towards Seringapatam. It was determined, if possible, to prevent this junction, and on the 10th August a body of Mysore Horse under Rama Row was despatched with this object. About thirty miles from Mysore Rama Row met the Chittledrug detachment and had an interview with Captain Mackintosh, who was in command, and to whom he intimated that he had instructions to use all means to prevent the further advance of the detachment. Captain Mackintosh replied that for his part he was determined not to be the first to attack, and he halted his men for the night. Unfortunately fresh letters urging immediate advance were received from the mutineers, and it was determined to push on at once. The sepoys were told that Purniah was attacking the Fort and that they were marching to its relief. The appearance of the Mysore Horse seemed to confirm this story.

The march was continued at 10 p.m., and on the morning of the 11th August, the Mysoreans attacked, but they were kept off without great difficulty. At about 11 a.m. news of the approach of the detachment reached the British encampment near Seringapatam and firing was heard in the distance. Colonel Gibbs then sent a squadron of Dragoons and the Light Infantry Company of H.M.'s 59th to endeavour to intercept the Chittledrug body, but without success, as the deep nullahs which intersected the country impeded the progress of the English force. An officer of the 59th was next ordered to advance under a white flag, but by some unexplained misapprehension he was fired on and slightly wounded. The Dragoons, who had now come up with the detachment, were then ordered to attack. The sepoys are alleged to have at first supposed that the Dragoons were friends. When they discovered their mistake, they broke and fled, protected partly by the nullahs, until they reached the shelter of the Fort. Many were cut down, killed or wounded. Captain Mackintosh, who was in command, was among the wounded and was made a prisoner. Another British officer, Lieutenant Best, died from fatigue. The whole of the baggage of the unfortunate detachment was captured, as well as two guns and the flags of at least one regiment. The exact loss of life was not accurately determined. The number of killed was returned as 9, but there were 281 missing, most of whom were probably slain, and there were 153 wounded. Less than 700 survivors entered Seringapatam. The British had no casualties.

The garrison in the Fort made but half-hearted attempts to intervene on behalf of the unfortunate fugitives from Chittledrug. A few shots were fired from the Fort, and a force of infantry under Lieutenant-Colonel Munro, with two companies of artillery and ten guns, marched out and threatened the British camp, which was guarded by the 5th Native Cavalry. But no serious attack was made and the force withdrew when fired on. That night, however, the guns in the Fort opened a heavy cannonade which necessitated the camp being shifted, though it served no useful purpose. The only victims were an unfortunate grasscutter and four horses.

Colonel Bell's proceedings in other respects were equally futile. He again wrote to Purniah trying to secure his neutrality, but without result. He sent a letter to the Rani of Coorg, asking her to facilitate the march through her territory of troops coming from Cannanore, although these troops did not appear. He addressed several further letters to the Governor-General, giving an account of the attack on the Chittledrug detachment, and endeavouring to throw on the Government forces the responsibility for that lamentable affair.

As the garrison in Seringapatam had, on the morning of the 11th, expressed a wish for a conference, Lieutenant-Colonel Davis on the 13th sent Lieutenant Greaves of His Majesty's 8th Regiment with a flag of truce to the Fort. He was admitted, after a long parley, and was conducted to the Town Major's office. There he was received by Colonel Bell and a number of other officers. As he reported afterwards, there seemed to be no control. Everyone was allowed to give his opinion. Almost all the officers present indulged in denunciations of the conduct of the loyal troops, and it was difficult to hear what was said owing to the "clamour of revilings and complaints." However, he brought back an answer from Colonel Bell saying that two officers would be sent next day to meet any two deputed from the camp. At 10 a.m. on the 14th August, Colonel Gibbs of His Majesty's 59th Regiment and Colonel G. P. Adams of His Majesty's 25th Dragoons met Lieutenant-Colonel Munro and Captain de Havilland at the fourth milestone on the Bangalore road. Much vague conversation passed. The delegates from the Fort declared Colonel Bell's inflexible resolution not to surrender except on the order of Lord Minto, and it was agreed that a despatch from the garrison to Lord Minto should be allowed to pass. Otherwise this interview seems to have met with no result.

During the next few days, both sides remained inactive, but on the 18th August, Mr. Cole received from Captain Sydenham the news of the submission of the Secunderabad officers and the letter which those officers had sent advising Colonel Bell and his associates to follow their example. Mr. Cole at first hesitated to open further communications with the Fort without the orders of Government. On the 20th, however, news reached him that the troops in Travancore intended to march to the relief of Seringapatam. He determined, therefore, to lose no time, and he sent into the Fort the letter from Secunderabad. This produced an immediate effect. On the morning of the 21st, two officers, Captain de Havilland and Captain Cadell, with a flag of truce, arrived in camp. They announced that an address to the Governor-General similar to that drawn up by the Secunderabad officers was under preparation in the Fort, and they asked that all hostile action should be suspended until it was ready. To this Lieutenant-Colonel Davis and Mr. Cole replied that the essential thing required to be done was not the preparation of addresses, but the surrender of the Fort, and the officers returned with this intimation. Next day Colonel Bell forwarded to Colonel Davis the Test subscribed by all the officers of the Company's regiments in the Fort, fifty-four in number. It was accompanied by an address to the Governor-General resembling that prepared at Secunderabad. In it they said that they had refused to sign the Test before "from the state of alarm they were then in, occasioned by the manner in which the paper was tendered to them by Lieutenant-Colonel Davis, by the various reports then prevalent, and by the horrible prospect open to them of being employed against their brother officers," many of whom were actually their relations. They appealed for a general amnesty. In sending this address Colonel Bell announced his willingness to surrender the Fort of Seringapatam, but claimed that the sepoys should not be dishonoured by being disarmed and should be allowed to march out with their arms. To this request Colonel Davis gave an emphatic refusal. He demanded that all arms should be piled in the Fort and that the sepoys should surrender absolutely unconditionally. After some hesitation this was accepted, and on the morning of the 23rd August the sepoys marched out, and were encamped not far from the Fort, which was at once occupied by Colonel Davis with three companies of the King's 59th Regiment.

CHAPTER XX

AFTER THE MUTINY

WITH the surrender of the Fort of Seringapatam on the 23rd August the mutiny may be said to have come to an end, having lasted just two months. A few isolated corps held out for a week or so longer. In the Northern Division the malcontent officers did not all sign the Test till the 30th August; at Palamcottah it was not accepted till the 31st, and at the West Coast until the 2nd September. Even then the Government did not relax its precautions. It was decided on the 6th September to maintain a "disposable Field Force" in the Southern Districts so as to be ready for all emergencies. Colonel Conran's army was meantime advancing in the Deccan, and on the 14th September a force of 1500 horse under the Mysorean Commander Ram Row was moving from Mysore towards Cumbum to join Colonel Conran. The officers of the Hyderabad Subsidiary Force at Secunderabad and Jaulna, though they had signed the Test, had done so only on compulsion and were still with their regiments, and therefore a potential source of danger.

As a practical question, however, the crisis was over. The mutiny had collapsed, thanks to the energetic measures taken by Sir George Barlow, and all that remained to be done was to allot punishment. On the 13th September the Governor-General, Lord Minto, landed at Madras and took over the conduct of affairs. He had sailed from Calcutta on the 5th August, but his passage had been delayed by the monsoon. With praiseworthy expedition he published his conclusions on the mutiny in a General Order of the 25th September, 1809. His decisions were marked by great leniency. Three officers only were ordered forthwith to be tried by court-martial, namely, Lieutenant-Colonel Bell, Major Storey and Lieutenant-Colonel Doveton. Eighteen others were given a choice between standing a court-martial and being dismissed the Service. All the rest, whether officers or men, were granted an amnesty and were restored to their former rank and position. A special feature of the Governor-General's decision was that no representative of the Secunderabad garrison was included in the list of officers selected for punishment. They were accorded this special degree of leniency on the ground that they had been the first to set the example of submission to the Government.

There then followed the dreary process of trying the guilty officers. Colonel John Bell's case was taken first. The court-martial began at Bangalore on the 1st November, 1809. It was composed of eighteen officers, of whom nine belonged to the King's Service and nine to Native Infantry Regiments. The prisoner objected to two of the former, and the third not having arrived, the trial actually took place with only fifteen officers, of whom six were in the King's and nine in the Company's service. The charge against the prisoner was that of mutiny and sedition, including firing upon the loyal troops, and on those of Mysore, seizing the Treasury and refusing to yield the Fort and garrison to the proper authorities. The hearing proceeded in a leisurely manner and actually occupied twelve days. On the 9th December the Court found the prisoner guilty, and he was sentenced to be cashiered, and was declared for ever unworthy of serving the Company in any military capacity whatever. The leniency of the sentence was regarded as extraordinary. Under military law a soldier guilty of mutiny was liable to capital punishment, and only a few years before this, sentence was not merely passed but executed on a number of men whose offences had been far less heinous than those of Colonel Bell. The Commander-in-Chief therefore intervened and called upon the court-martial to revise their sentence, but they refused. This did not take place till 27th February, 1810, and there was now nothing for it but to confirm the finding, and this was done on 8th March, the Commander-in-Chief recording his "pointed disapprobation" of the punishment awarded to the prisoner, which, he said, was altogether disproportionate to the crimes proved against him.

The second court-martial, that of Major Joseph Storey, did not begin until 8th January, the Court being composed of eight King's Officers and eight officers belonging to Native Infantry Regiments. The trial was conducted more expeditiously, but the result was much the same. Major Storey was found guilty of mutiny in having placed his Commanding Officer under arrest, assumed command of the garrison of Masulipatam, and issued the address of the 7th August to the Governor-General. He too was sentenced to be cashiered, but the further clause declaring him unfit to be ever re-employed in the Company's service was omitted, and the Court sent a letter to the Commander-in-Chief specially recommending the prisoner to mercy. As before, the Commander-in-Chief pointed out that the sentence passed was inadequate, but the Court refused to reconsider it, and it also was finally confirmed.

On the 26th January, 1810, the same Court tried Lieutenant-Colonel Doveton. The charges against him were somewhat differently framed, but the purport was much the same. The prisoner was charged with abandoning his post and moving his detachment from Jaulna "with a mutinous and seditious design against the existing Government of Fort St. George." He was further charged with having endeavoured to stir up and excite the troops to join in mutiny and sedition, and with having signed the mutinous and seditious paper called the Declaration. After a short trial the Court on the 5th February found the prisoner not guilty of the charges brought against him, and acquitted him "in the most full and honourable manner." Once more the Commander-in-Chief intervened, requesting the Court to reconsider its verdict, and for the third time the Court refused. Colonel Doveton had to be released from arrest, but the Governor-General suspended him from all military functions, though allowing him to draw the pay and allowances of his rank.

Two more officers, Lieutenant-Colonel Robert Munro and Major Kenny, both belonging to the Seringapatam garrison, were subsequently tried by court-martial, found guilty, and ordered to be cashiered. The remaining officers who had elected to stand their trial changed their minds and requested to be dismissed. The results of these trials were not much to the liking of the authorities. They would have preferred to exercise the quality of mercy themselves, instead of seeing this graceful function appropriated by the courts-martial. Lord Minto wrote to his wife, in tones of annoyance, that they had been "very soft," and had thrown on the Government the odium of pressing for more severe sentences. But the truth was that the officers who sat on these courts-martial had far too much sympathy with the mutineers to sentence them to capital punishment. Even to the King's officers there were many appealing circumstances about the affair, and to those members of the Courts who were themselves in the Company's service it was not to be expected that they would condemn those who had been but the other day friends and comrades. If the Government had wished to secure severe convictions and "salutary examples" they would have had to pack the Courts very carefully. No one really wanted to punish these officers very severely. The amnesty granted to the great bulk of the guilty showed that quite clearly; and it would have been an act of undoubted harshness to make scapegoats of the leaders, who had conspicuously failed to lead.

In the end, the great majority of the twenty-one officers who were excepted from the amnesty got back to the Service and finished their careers without the episode of 1809 having had any very serious effect. Colonel John Bell was never restored. It was felt apparently that a man who had fired on British troops and whose action had involved the death of some 400 sepoys had gone a little too far to be re-employed. The two officers who had led the unfortunate detachment from Chittledrug were also never restored to the service. On them, too, the guilt of innocent blood remained. Captain James Patterson, who had been concerned in the seizure of the Treasury at Cocanada and in other acts of violence in the Rajahmundry district, was also not restored. All the rest, except one who died before his trial came on, were eventually reinstated. A list will be found at the end of this chapter.

With the courts-martial the story of the mutiny comes to an end. The agitation in the Army did not, however, immediately disappear. Officers who had supported the Government or who had signed the Test were subjected to a considerable amount of petty persecution, being sent to Coventry and excluded from all social life and amenities. The officers belonging to the Company's service refused to have anything to do with the King's regiments, by which they said they had been "betrayed." Critics differed as to the future course of events. Some, such as

Lieutenant-Colonel Malcolm, declared that the Madras Army had been so treated that it was out of any man's power to avert the consequences which must arise from the measures taken by Sir George Barlow.[1] Others considered that Lord Minto had been as much too lenient as Barlow had been too severe. General Maitland sent home from Ceylon alarming reports of the state of insubordination among the officers. Eventually, however, both classes of critics proved to be wrong. With the lapse of time, quiet gradually supervened. The Army settled down to orderly methods again, until the excitement of 1809 was not merely allowed to die out, it was forgotten.

[1] Letter to Lord Wellesley dated 14th Sept. 1809: Wellesley MSS., Vol. 13637.

List of Officers selected for Punishment in the Governor-General's Order of 25th September, 1809, with eventual Disposal.

		Governor-General's Order.	Result of Court-martial.	Subsequent History.
1. Lieutenant-Colonel John Bell, of Madras Artillery.	Commanding Fort of Seringapatam.	To be tried by Court-martial.	Sentenced to be cashiered and incapable of re-employment.	Cashiered 8th March, 1810. Not restored.
2. Major Joseph Storey, of the 19th Native Infantry.	Commanding Battalion at Masulipatam.	Ditto.	Sentenced to be cashiered but recommended to mercy.	Cashiered. Restored to service (1817). Afterwards Lieutenant-Colonel. Died 1818.
3. Lieutenant-Colonel John Doveton, 7th Regiment Native Cavalry.	Commanding Detachment at Jaulna.	Ditto.	Acquitted.	Dismissed by Court of Directors. Restored to service (1813). Afterwards Lieutenant-General and G.C.B.
4. Lieutenant-Colonel Robert Munro, 15th Regiment Native Infantry.	Commanding Battalion at Seringapatam.	Option between Court-martial and dismissal.	Elected to take his trial. Sentenced to be cashiered.	Cashiered. Restored to service (1814). Died 1817.
5. Major D. C. Kenny, 19th Regiment Native Infantry.	Ditto.	Ditto.	Ditto.	Cashiered. Restored to service (1814). Afterwards Lieutenant-General. Died 1847.
6. Captain T. F. De Havilland, Engineers.	At Seringapatam.	Ditto.	Ditto.	Dismissed. Restored to service. Afterwards Lieutenant-Colonel. Retired 1825. Died 1866.

7. Captain George Cadell, 12th Regiment Native Infantry.	Town Major, Seringapatam.	Option between Court-martial and dismissal.	At first elected to be tried: later accepted dismissal.	Dismissed. Restored to service. Afterwards Lieutenant-Colonel. Retired 1827.
8. Captain Hugh McIntosh, 8th Regiment Native Infantry.	Commanding Detachment at Chittledrug.	Ditto.	Ditto.	Dismissed. Not restored.
9. Captain F. K. Aiskill, 15th Regiment Native Infantry.	Ditto.	Ditto.	Ditto.	Dismissed. Not restored.
10. Captain Augustus Andrews, Madras European Regiment.	At Masulipatam.	Ditto.	Ditto.	Dismissed. Restored. Afterwards Major-General and C.B.
11. Captain James Patterson, 11th Regiment Native Infantry.	Commanding at Samulkottah.	Ditto.	Accepted alternative of dismissal.	Dismissed. Not restored.
12. Captain George Wahab, 21st Regiment Native Infantry.	Second in Command at Chicacole.	Ditto.	Ditto.	Dismissed. Restored. Afterwards Major-General. Died 1843.
13. Captain James Sadler, 24th Regiment Native Infantry.	At Ellore.	Ditto.	Ditto.	Dismissed. Restored (1814). Killed in action near Nagpur, 27th November, 1817.
14. Captain J. L. Lushington, 4th Regiment Native Cavalry.	At Jaulna.	Ditto.	At first elected to take his trial: later accepted dismissal.	Dismissed. Restored. Afterwards General and G.C.B., also Director of E.I. Co.

LIST OF OFFICERS SELECTED FOR PUNISHMENT IN THE GOVERNOR-GENERAL'S ORDER OF 25TH SEPTEMBER, 1809, WITH EVENTUAL DISPOSAL (*continued*).

		Governor-General's Order.	Result of Court-martial.	Subsequent History.
15. Captain Alexander McCleod, 8th Regiment Native Cavalry.	At Jaulna.	Option between Court-martial and dismissal.	Accepted alternative of dismissal.	Dismissed. Restored. Afterwards Lieutenant-Colonel. Died 1825.
16. Captain Chas. Hopkinson, Artillery.	At Jaulna.	Ditto.	Ditto.	Dismissed. Restored. Afterwards Lieutenant-Colonel and C.B. Retired 1829.
17. Captain G. W. Poignand, Artillery.	At Jaulna.	Ditto.	Ditto.	Dismissed. Restored (1814). Died 1820.
18. Captain G. M. Gibson, 10th Regiment Native Infantry.	At Jaulna.	Ditto.	Ditto.	Dismissed. Restored. Afterwards Major. Died 1814.
19. Captain Thomas Pollak, 12th Regiment Native Infantry.	At Jaulna.	Ditto.	At first elected to take his trial : later accepted dismissal.	Dismissed. Restored. Afterwards Major-General and C.B.
20. Major Matthew Stewart, 17th Regiment Native Infantry.	At Jaulna.	Ditto.	Accepted alternative of dismissal.	Dismissed. Restored (1814). Afterwards Lieutenant-Colonel. Died 1818.
21. Captain John Turner, 15th Regiment Native Infantry.	At Seringapatam.	Ditto.	Died on 23rd October, 1809.	

CHAPTER XXI

CONCLUSION

An event so extraordinary, if not unique, as a wholesale mutiny of British officers may well require some clear explanation. That it was not due to the grievances of the Army seems beyond doubt. These related to such everyday affairs as promotion and allowances and, as General John Briggs wrote in 1842, they were "partial and in some measure unreal."[1] Nor can the outbreak be truly ascribed to the measures taken by Sir George Barlow. He was denounced and detested long before he had taken any action at all against the Army. The outbreak must rather be ascribed to deeper and more general causes.

Madras was, as we have seen, in a thoroughly unwholesome state at the beginning of the nineteenth century. Faction was rife, and there was a spirit of licence abroad which was the result of a long period of lax government and of intemperate attacks on authority. The Army was equally permeated by a spirit of insubordination. The memories of the past, of the Bengal mutiny of 1766, and of the overthrow of Lord Pigott mingled with the consciousness of the successful agitations of later years when concessions had been wrung from an unwilling Court of Directors in London. Such lessons were bad for any army, but

[1] A Letter on the Indian Army, May, 1842, by General J. Briggs.

most of all for one not yet fortified by long-established traditions of military discipline.

Moreover, the military reorganization of 1796, while it had conferred great benefits on the Indian Army, had brought with it certain dangers. It had suddenly introduced so great an influx of new officers as to swamp the authority of the seniors. Out of a total strength, including cadets, of about 1450 officers, only 156 were above the rank of Captain. The rest were young men, largely under the age of twenty-five, and meriting Malcolm's description of them as "a set of mad-headed boys."[1] In a not dissimilar estimate Lord Minto refers to the mutinous officers as mostly "very young and half-instructed men, brought together in a distant corner of the Empire and removed from the influence of that public opinion which exists in all large and mixed societies."[2]

The Madras Army, thus composed, was placed towards the close of 1807 under the command of General Macdowall, an officer suffering under a sense of personal grievance. Lord Minto believed that General Macdowall has conscientiously worked "with infinite industry, and no inconsiderable skill,"[3] to foment discontent in the Army. It seems more probable, however, that the mischief which the General's character and conduct undoubtedly did was

[1] Letter to Lord Minto dated 15th June, 1809.

[2] Lord Minto's Letter to the Court of Directors dated 27th May, 1810.

[3] Lord Minto's Letter to the Secret Committee dated 5th February, 1810.

unintentional. Weak, vain and loquacious, he did not realize how dangerous his words and example were to the excitable young men by whom he was surrounded, or how far he had guided the Army on the road to mutiny before he left the country. Even so early as the month of January 1809, wild talk of putting the Governor in a masulah boat and sending him over the surf was prevalent. This is proved by contemporary letters [1] as well as by the later vapourings of retired veterans.[2]

The steps taken by Sir George Barlow to restore discipline in the Army cannot be all defended, but they furnish an inadequate explanation of the extraordinary hatred with which he came to be regarded. Reactions from the civil disputes of the time, the influence of men like Petrie, Roebuck, Parry, Marsh and others, must be allowed for, and Barlow's reputation as an advocate of reform and retrenchment doubtless helped. At a later stage the hatred of him became an obsession. He was habitually referred to as a tyrant and a villain. "Oh, great God," cries Major Poignand, "I know no name too bad for him." [3] Lieutenant-Colonel Malcolm writes of the officers as having "acted under the influence of temporary insanity." [4] Such a description cannot be said to be

[1] See Sir E. Pellew's letter dated 15th February, 1809, in Appendix D.

[2] See Diary of Colonel Charles Bayly, 12th Suffolk Regiment, 1796–1830.

[3] See Letter No. 15 in Appendix F.

[4] Wellesley MSS., Vol. 13637. Letter dated 25th August, 1809, to Lord Minto.

too strong for the state of mind of the great majority who were concerned in the mutiny.

No enterprise of such serious moment was indeed ever entered upon with more light-hearted recklessness. No leader was appointed, no programme drawn up, no agreed plan of operations laid down. Wild excitement prevailed everywhere, but no one knew what was to be the object in view. Vague plans of marching on Madras and seizing the person of Sir George Barlow were combined with protestations of loyalty to the Company and Crown and of undying patriotism.

It was characteristic of this mutiny without method that no serious attempt seems to have been made to secure the adhesion, or even the neutrality, of the King's regiments. In August 1809 a highly rhetorical appeal to "The Officers of His Majesty's Regiments" was posted from a remote station in the south of the Presidency, but this seems to have been the work of some individual genius more wide awake than his fellows. It came too late to have any effect.

Yet the attitude of the British troops was evidently the crux of the situation. It was not to be supposed that the officers of the Company's Army would lead their troops against British regiments, or that the sepoys would follow them if they were to lead. The sepoy had indeed no real interest in the quarrel. It made no difference to him whether General Macdowall had a seat in Council or whether his officers got Bengal allowances or not. He was simply "a large-family man" on the meagre pay of Rs. 7 a month, and there was no reason at all why he should get himself killed in a cause which was not his and in which he had everything to lose and nothing to gain.

It was the knowledge that the sepoy was not prepared to go into the field in support of his officers that brought about the collapse of the mutiny. The enemies of Sir George Barlow pretended that it was the news of Lord Minto's approaching visit which made the mutineers at Secunderabad surrender, but Captain John Orrok, who was actually there at the time, is a witness to the contrary. "The Governor," he wrote, "instantly despatched men-of-war to Bombay and Ceylon, and in a short time they returned with 5000 men, King's Regiments. These were encamped near Madras, and the Company's officers, finding that the sepoys would never stand a fight against Europeans, began to think they had carried matters too far."[1] This contemporary evidence as to the true causes of the surrender has only lately been made available.

When the mutiny was over, the treatment of the guilty parties seems to have been marked by moderation and sound judgment. No one wished to see men who had been led into the crime of mutiny more by schoolboy excitement than by any deep-laid schemes or criminal ambitions—no one could wish to see them sentenced to capital punishment. It was amply sufficient to get rid of a few of the most violent. But there can be no doubt that this mutiny and its ignominious termination gave the Army a useful lesson.

[1] *Letters of John Orrok*, p. 111.

It is no slight thing to encourage a large body of men with arms in their hands to attempt the subversion of the civil government. If the attempt had succeeded it must have exercised a most harmful effect on the discipline and moral of the Indian Army for at least a generation.

The man who met and defeated the mutiny was undoubtedly Sir George Barlow. It was said at the time that he had saved the British Empire in India from the greatest danger it had ever encountered. The statement was true, and it was an achievement which ought never to be forgotten. But the force of faction in those days was so great that within three or four years the lesson of the mutiny was lost sight of, Sir George Barlow was recalled, and all the measures which he had taken reversed. Nothing could be a clearer proof of the inherent weakness of the system which laid the fortunes of India at the mercy of the votes of a shifting body of merchants in Leadenhall Street.

APPENDICES

APPENDIX A

THE SUPREME COURT

UP to the year 1798 the administration of civil justice in the city of Madras was entrusted to a Court, presided over by the Mayor and composed of the Mayor and Aldermen, which was known as the Mayor's Court. In that year a new Court, known as the Recorder's Court, took the place of the old Mayor's Court, and on the 28th September, 1798, Sir Thomas Strange,[1] who had been seven years Chief Justice of Nova Scotia, arrived in Madras and took up the office of Recorder on a salary of Rs. 5000 *per mensem*.

The Mayor of Madras had been a certain European merchant, Mr. William Abbott, and he and his partner, Mr. Benjamin Roebuck, who combined trade and an official position as Master of the Mint, were not too pleased to see the old Court which they had controlled disappear. But under the new constitution a certain number of aldermen were to sit by rotation, as judges in the Recorder's Court, and Mr. Abbott and his friends at once set to work to try and capture the new Court and the Recorder.

The opposition began within the first term, and in

[1] Sir Thomas Strange (1756–1841), knighted March 1798, retired 1817: author of *Elements of Hindu Law*. A fine portrait of him by Shee hangs in Christchurch Hall, Oxford.

a letter[1] dated 12th February, 1799, to the President of the Board of Control, Sir Thomas Strange described the difficulties which he had had to face. Messrs. Abbott and Roebuck, supported by other aldermen, had done their best to "counteract" the new constitution. Among other matters, they had tried to get established an extravagant scale of fees which was intended to benefit young Abbott, who was Deputy Registrar of the Court. They had also put forward a claim to take a part in all the Recorder's letters to the Government, an arrangement which, Sir Thomas Strange wrote, would have been inconvenient on account of "their decided and avowed enmity to the Government." In fact he regarded the scheme of the Recorder's Court, with its element of aldermen judges, as quite unworkable. Some of the members of the Corporation, he said, "had been shameless in endeavouring to pervert their trust to their own private ends." The rest were unfitted for judicial functions by reason of their business ties and connections. He recommended that a new Act should be passed constituting a new Court from which the commercial element would be entirely eliminated.

Sir Thomas Strange's account of the position is fully corroborated by a letter from Mr. Benjamin Sulivan, who had been Advocate-General for the last twenty years. "Sir Thomas Strange," this letter said, "is a man of mild manners, and with any other set of men would have got on very quietly, but Messrs. Roebuck and Abbott endeavoured to throw him into

[1] India Office Records: Home, Miscellaneous, Vol. 430.

the background, to engross the patronage to themselves, and to increase the fees of Mr. Taylor, the principal officer of the Court, with a view to the future emolument of young Abbott, his present Deputy."[1]

Sir Thomas Strange succeeded in holding his own, and in October 1799 he wrote that the Recorder's Court was now working better, but that the system was inherently bad, and that a change in constitution was indispensable. A seat in the Mayor's Court, he said, used to be sought by some as giving a certain status and influence among natives, and by others "for purposes of sordid and corrupt profit"; now that the control was exercised by the Recorder, the aldermen no longer cared to serve as judges and often declined a seat.

The representations thus made had effect. By Statute 39 and 40 George III, c. 79, the Recorder's Court was in its turn superseded by a Supreme Court composed of a Chief Justice and two Puisne Judges. Sir Thomas Strange was the first Chief Justice, and the two Judges were Mr., afterwards Sir, Benjamin Sulivan and Sir Henry Gwillim.

The new Supreme Court was established from 2nd September, 1801. Quarrels began at once. At the first Sessions, Sir Henry Gwillim expressed dissatisfaction with the procedure, and at his instance, Sir Thomas Strange wrote to the Chief Justice of Calcutta, Sir John Anstruther, asking how matters were carried on there. This inquiry was made in a private

[1] India Office Records: Home, Miscellaneous, Vol. 430.

letter, and Sir John Anstruther's reply was couched in informal terms. Sir Thomas Strange sent an extract to Sir Henry Gwillim. But this gentleman took mortal offence at some careless phrase in which Sir John Anstruther spoke of "throwing" cases to his Puisne Judges. Gwillim sent Sir Thomas Strange on 19th December, 1801, a long letter full of sarcastic and angry comment, and when Strange asked him to return the extract from Sir John Anstruther's letter, he not only refused to return it, but told the Chief Justice in rude terms that he knew he ought not to have made such a request. Sir Henry Gwillim ended by saying that his engagements obliged him to decline any further epistolary communication with Sir Thomas Strange.

The relations which commenced in so unpromising a manner were not likely to improve with time. Sir Henry Gwillim possessed a peculiarly offensive and violent style of writing, and from the first he made no attempt to restrain himself in his communications with the Chief Justice. Sir Thomas Strange, on the other hand, was, as Mr. Sulivan had remarked, "a man of mild manners," and he seems to have gone to great lengths in the attempt to conciliate his overbearing and difficult colleague.

Early in 1805, Sir Thomas Strange proceeded to England, with the object, it seems, of laying before the authorities there some further proposals relating to the Court. He returned to Madras on the 28th June, 1806, and on the same day he went to call on Sir Henry Gwillim. He saw Lady Gwillim and had a long talk with her, leaving his card on her husband, who did not appear. Next day Sir Henry Gwillim sent a Mr. Clarke, who was employed by him in a secretarial capacity, to interview the Chief Justice and to inform him that Sir Henry Gwillim could not return the Chief Justice's call " in consequence of the indignity he had received " by the Chief Justice's going to England without telling him the objects of his visit. Sir Thomas Strange, who throughout showed admirable temper and self-restraint, then wrote Sir Henry Gwillim a friendly letter expressing the hope that relations might be renewed. Sir Henry Gwillim refused to reply and again sent his secretary, Mr. Clarke, to communicate his refusal. Sir Thomas Strange made another effort to make peace. He suggested that he should meet Sir Henry Gwillim at Mr. Justice Sulivan's chambers. To this, however, Sulivan demurred. He had been present, he said, at one scene " of disgusting intemperance " and did not wish to witness a second. Such, he said, is " the unhappiness of Sir Henry's disposition that the violence of his temper gets completely the better of his reason." All communication between the Chief Justice and Sir Henry Gwillim thus ceased.

During Sir Thomas Strange's absence in England, Sir Henry Gwillim had quarrelled with the Government. As regards the Governor, Lord William Bentinck, he declared that his conduct had been such that Gwillim " could never be on terms with him " again. The senior member of Council, Mr. Petrie, had also affronted him by giving a dinner to which he was not invited. Altogether the Government had treated him in a disgraceful manner.

To this private quarrel an official quarrel was now added. The two Puisne Judges had written to Government while Sir Thomas Strange was away, asking for some establishment. Correspondence on this subject continued after the Chief Justice's return, and on the 15th November, 1806, the Government returned a letter signed by the two Puisne Judges in order that it might also receive the authentication of the Chief Justice. This step was deeply resented by Sir Henry Gwillim, and both he and Sulivan declined to hold any communication with the Government until the insulting letter had been withdrawn.

In July 1806 the mutiny had occurred at Vellore. It was believed that the conspiracy had been widespread and had broken out at Vellore prematurely, and the Government thought it necessary, therefore, to create a Police Force in Madras, where hitherto there had been no custodians of the peace except a few watchmen and peons under a Polygar or hereditary Hindu officer.[1] A force of regular police was now enlisted and placed under the control of a Mr. W. Grant.

Sir Henry Gwillim professed to see in this new Police an engine of official oppression. He belonged apparently to that section of the Whig party which had imbibed the principles of the French Revolution and were full of strange Jacobin doctrine. Hence his extravagant opposition to the new force of police. The monsoon had failed and food prices were rising;

[1] India Office Records: Home, Miscellaneous, Vol. 691.

and rioting broke out in the grain bazar. When the Government used the police to put down this rioting, Sir Henry Gwillim had the policemen arrested and forced the sentinels placed in the bazars to be withdrawn. The Superintendent of Police whereupon resigned, and the Government appointed in his place, Captain James Grant.

This appointment drove Sir Henry Gwillim to a state of fury. On the 21st January, 1807, in his Charge to the Grand Jury, he denounced "the repeated insults which had been offered to himself and Sir Benjamin Sulivan by the Government and by the very ill-advised young gentleman at the head of it." Among the insults he had received was the action of the Government in returning the Puisne Judges' letter on 15th November, 1806, the introduction of the new police without consulting the Supreme Court, and the proposed institution of a Legislative Council to make laws and regulations. He violently attacked the action of the police and he threatened that they should be proceeded against criminally. His Charge was reported to Government by the Advocate-General, Mr. Anstruther,[1] with whom also Sir Henry Gwillim was on terms of bitter hostility.

In February 1807 the Government ordered the Superintendent of Police to arrest an Indian against whom a criminal charge was made, and this was done. One of Sir Henry Gwillim's friends was a barrister named Charles Marsh, and motion for Habeas Corpus was made by him on behalf of the arrested Indian.

[1] Afterwards Sir Alexander Anstruther and Recorder of Bombay.

At the hearing of this motion, Sir Henry Gwillim burst out into abuse of the Government, and especially of the Governor. "Can these outrages," he said, "be sanctioned by a Bentinck, by one of that family so illustrious in the cause of liberty? It is impossible! None of the noble blood of the Cavendishes can flow in the veins of this man. He must be some spurious changeling that has been palmed (off) upon that noble family and contaminated it. . . . What! put a soldier to act at the head of the police where he is to deprive men of their liberties? . . . Not one of us is safe. We are living under a complete military despotism." He attacked Mr. Anstruther for having reported what he had said, and a little later he suggested to Mr. Marsh that he should move for an attachment against Captain Grant for not making a sufficient return to the Habeas Corpus. When the Advocate-General applied for copies of the affidavits on which the writ of Habeas Corpus was issued, Sir Henry Gwillim again denounced Mr. Anstruther, vowing that his conduct in advising the Government to make such an application should not pass with impunity, and saying that he was determined to bring it "before the twelve Judges." The violence of his language throughout all these proceedings suggested a state of mental derangement.

Sir Henry Gwillim was not, however, satisfied by these extraordinary outbursts on the Bench; he seems also to have attempted direct interference with the police, for a police peon was dismissed by the Superintendent for having conducted Sir Henry Gwillim's Secretary, Mr. Clarke, to the Darogah's house. Sir

Henry Gwillim then obtained a petition from this dismissed policeman and sent it to the Chief Secretary, with a letter in which he said that if the Government did not give satisfaction, he would submit the matter to His Majesty's Ministers, that His Majesty might know the spirit and character of the new police at this place, adding many other extravagant remarks.[1]

It was, of course, impossible to allow such language on the part of a Judge of the Supreme Court to pass unnoticed, and the Government accordingly proposed to address the Court of Directors. Before doing so, they asked Sir Henry Gwillim if he wished to submit any explanation. To this he merely returned an insolent reply, in which he spoke of the Advocate-General, who had reported his language, as an informer, declared that the Government would have to explain their conduct in starting "the cumbrous and expensive police," and in appointing a military man "to the direction of that offensive machine." When the Government had done all that he would be quite ready to explain his conduct.

At each Sessions further scenes occurred. When on the 10th July, 1807, Mr. Anstruther attended to hear Sir Henry Gwillim's address to the Grand Jury, Sir Henry Gwillim addressed him by name and abused him, saying: "You are destitute of all proper feelings. You deserve to be kicked out of your profession. You are a contemptible fellow." Another day, noticing Mr. Anstruther smile, Sir Henry Gwillim burst out: "Sir, do not presume to laugh at me.

[1] India Office Records: Home, Miscellaneous, Vol. 691.

If I again see a smile on your countenance I shall immediately commit you."

In consequence of Sir Henry Gwillim's conduct on the Bench, the Government wrote to the Chief Justice, requesting him to sit with Sir Henry Gwillim so as to impose some restraint on his extravagances. This the Chief Justice did. Sir Henry Gwillim had again attacked the police in his Charge. When the Chief Justice arrived, Gwillim retired, and the Chief Justice then addressed the Grand Jury himself, and told them that the Government had done quite right in creating the police, that the police had generally behaved well, and that the Superintendent's conduct had been moderate and judicious. If the Government had not created an efficient police, after what had happened at Vellore, they would have been guilty of a grave neglect of duty.

But Madras juries in those days were apparently swayed by motives which cannot now be understood, and the Grand Jury presented a finding that Captain James Grant, as Superintendent of Police, had exercised military power in Madras by arresting persons without lawful authority or warrant, and they considered this action to be against the law and the Constitution. The Advocate-General said that in view of their finding, the Grand Jury should proceed to an indictment of Captain Grant. The foreman refused, saying their reasons were not positive. Sir Henry Gwillim said that the Jury could not be forced to proceed and called on Mr. Marsh, who said he was not ready to proceed. The Chief Justice thereupon ruled that the bill of indictment must be proceeded with, whereupon Sir Henry Gwillim violently attacked the Chief Justice on the Bench, and a painful scene followed.

Meantime the Government had some months before addressed the Court of Directors, forwarding the Advocate-General's reports of Sir Henry Gwillim's extraordinary language and behaviour. The Court of Directors, on legal advice, presented a petition to the Crown, and on the 12th November, 1807, orders recalling Sir Henry Gwillim to England to furnish an explanation of his conduct were despatched. But communications were slow in those days and the order of recall did not reach Madras until June 1808. On the 29th June, 1808, Sir Henry Gwillim acknowledged the receipt of the order and announced that he would start for home in October, when the fleet, with convoy, would be sailing. Up to the last he maintained his strange conduct, delivering a violent attack on the Government in his last Charge to the Grand Jury. He sailed from Madras in October 1808, and on the 17th May, 1809, he reported his arrival in England after a seven months' voyage. Arrangements had already been made by the Board of Control for an inquiry into his conduct to be made by the Lords of the Privy Council, and in a letter dated the 11th April, 1810, the President of the Board informed the Chairman of the Court of Directors that His Majesty had been pleased to approve of a report from the Lords of the Privy Council respecting Sir Henry Gwillim's conduct, and had directed that Sir Henry

Gwillim should be "removed from his situation as one of the Puisne Judges of the Supreme Court of Judicature at Madras." Sir Henry Gwillim's career in the Madras High Court was thus ended, but the influence which his violent conduct and his defiance of Government had had on Madras could not be at once effaced. His henchman, Mr. Charles Marsh, remained and carried on the tradition of insurgency and obstruction with great activity during Sir George Barlow's tenure of office, returning eventually to England to continue the attack there.

APPENDIX B

THE QUESTION OF THE CARNATIC DEBTS

MUHAMMAD ALI, Nabob of the Carnatic, better known as the Nabob Wallajah, after the triumph of the English arms in Southern India, took up his residence at Madras, where he built himself a palace. He was a man of extravagant habits and he became more and more steeped in debt, both to the East India Company and to private creditors. To both he made over tracts of country as security for his debts, and his bonds were freely bought and sold, the discount on them falling or rising as the prospects of the Nabob's debts being liquidated became more or less favourable. All sorts of people, European and Indian, official and non-official, became interested in his debts, which came to exercise a demoralizing influence on society, as it became to the interest of different classes to support the vicious system of the management of whole districts by money-lending creditors.

The Nabob died in 1795, but the same state of things continued under his son and successor, Umdat-ul-Umara. In 1801, after the conquest of Mysore, Lord Wellesley determined to put an end to it. His action was slightly deferred by the Nabob Umdat-ul-Umara's illness and death, but in June 1801 his successor signed a treaty by which he practically made over the whole country to the Company, who, in return, undertook, among other things, to arrange for the liquidation of the Nabob's debts, an annual payment of 340,000 pagodas, or about £120,000, being set aside for the purpose. A deed of agreement was signed on 10th July, 1805, between the Company and the Nabob's creditors. Statutory power was taken to appoint three Commissioners sitting in London to adjudicate on all claims, while, for the purpose of local inquiry, the Governor-General appointed three Commissioners, servants of the Company on the Bengal Establishment, who were to investigate claims in India and report to the Commissioners in London. Thus a complete machinery was provided for examining the validity of all claims.

The Bengal Commissioners, Messrs. Parker, Goad and Russell, arrived in Madras in February 1808, and after necessary preliminaries they began their investigation. Being quite unconnected with South India they were free from all local prepossessions, and entitled therefore to the special confidence and support of the Government.

In May 1808, information reached the Government of the existence in Madras of large quantities of forged bonds purporting to have been signed by the Nabobs; and a Committee, presided over by the Advocate-General and including the Company's Solicitor, Mr. Orme, and two servants of the Company, Mr. W. Oliver and Captain F. Thompson, was appointed to trace the source of this information and to report whether it was true or not. The Committee reported that it was true that forged bonds existed to an enormous extent, and that forged entries in support of these bonds had been made in the Durbar books. The Committee added that attempts had been made to show that the Nabob's Sherishtadar, Roya Reddi Row, had played a leading part in introducing these forged entries, but that these attempts had totally failed, and were due to intrigue intended to secure Roya Reddi Row's removal from office. In a later report, the Committee added that a dubash, named A. Paupiah, who had been convicted some years before of conspiracy and sentenced to three years' imprisonment, a fine of £1000, and the pillory, was an active party in this intrigue against Roya Reddi Row, and that A. Paupiah was himself concerned in the forgery of a bond for 46,000 pagodas, and they recommended that he should be proceeded against for this offence. The Government accepted the Committee's report and sanctioned the prosecution of A. Paupiah.

Meantime the Bengal Commissioners had commenced their inquiry, and the first bond which they took up for investigation was one propounded by Roya Reddi Row. It was for 38,500 pagodas, and purported to be on account of a loan made to the Nabob by one Gopal Row, and it was in the handwriting of Reddi Row's brother, Ananda Row. A. Paupiah denounced the bond as a forgery and was supported by Mr. William Abbott, of the firm of Abbott, Roebuck and Maitland, and Mr. Thomas Parry, an English merchant, who some years before had been connected with A. Paupiah in an attempt to raise money for the Nabob in Tinnevelly, and had been ordered by the Court of Directors to leave India "as a warning to others not to engage in usurious loans."[1] After a long investigation, the Bengal Commissioners found that Paupiah's charges were false and Reddi Row's bond genuine, and they also recommended that Paupiah should be proceeded against for conspiracy and some of his witnesses for perjury.

Paupiah and his party, however, did not wait to be attacked, but promptly carried the war into the enemy's country. Finding that the Bengal Commissioners were against him, and in favour of the rival, Roya Reddi Row, Paupiah and his supporters decided to turn the Commissioners' flank by lodging a charge of forgery in the criminal courts against Roya Reddi Row. This was first attempted before a Justice of the Peace named Taswell, who declined to make the order desired. The application was then renewed before Mr. Maitland, who was Mr. Abbott's partner, sitting as a Justice of the Peace, and he, after a brief inquiry, committed Roya Reddi Row and his brother Ananda Row for trial before the Supreme Court on a charge of forgery of the deed for 38,500 pagodas, which the Bengal Commissioners had had under inquiry and had found to be genuine.

It was obvious that if the opponents of any deed on which the Bengal Commissioners adjudicated could immediately have recourse to the criminal courts to reverse their finding, the result would be to bring

[1] India Office Records: Home, Miscellaneous, Vol. 613.

their inquiry to a standstill until, in each case, the criminal courts had decided. The Legislature had not foreseen or provided for such a contingency, and the Commissioners found themselves in a grave difficulty. Meantime they moved the Government to instruct the law officers to assist in Roya Reddi Row's defence, which was done, and with still more doubtful wisdom they started a prosecution for perjury against two of the witnesses whom Paupiah had brought to give evidence before them against Roya Reddi Row and his bond, by name Bhima Row and Arunachella Row.

Meantime the men who were behind Paupiah in this matter, Messrs. Abbott, his partner Roebuck and Mr. Parry, opened a correspondence with Government, the object of which was to protest against the law officers being employed on Roya Reddi Row's side.

Their argument that the appearance of the law officers would deter native witnesses from coming forward in future to give evidence was not without plausibility, but the Government felt it their duty to support the Bengal Commissioners and refused to reconsider the orders already passed.

Events, however, developed in a manner wholly unexpected by the Government or the Bengal Commissioners. At the trial in the Supreme Court, Roya Reddi Row was found guilty by the Jury, although the Chief Justice, who presided, had summed up strongly in favour of the accused. Sir Thomas Strange was so strongly persuaded of the perverse character of the Jury's verdict that he refused to pass sentence. On the other hand, the two witnesses, Bhima Row and Arunachella Row, against whom the Bengal Commissioners had started proceedings, were acquitted. Moreover, fresh prosecutions which had been instituted by Paupiah and his group against Roya Reddi Row and Mr. J. Battley, Secretary to the Nabob, ended in the conviction of those persons, but once more the Chief Justice declined to pass sentence, and eventually referred these convictions to England, where they were quashed. For the present, however, the Bengal Commissioners had been defeated all along the line, and the Government, which had supported them, naturally shared in their discomfiture.

By the close of the year 1808, the party of A. Paupiah, which included Messrs. Abbott, Roebuck, R. A. Maitland and Thomas Parry, had succeeded so decisively in the law courts that they took further steps to enforce their victory. On the 5th January, Messrs. Abbott, Parry and R. A. Maitland sent to the Government of Madras for transmission to Bengal a Memorial addressed to the Governor-General in Council. This detailed the steps they had taken in connection with the prosecution of Roya Reddi Row, Ananda Row, and Mr. Battley, and asked that they might be reimbursed for all the expenses of those prosecutions. It also said that the Bengal Commissioners had "delivered themselves up to the law officers and their associates," and were thereby rendered unfit for the performance of their duties, and should be replaced by more competent persons. On the same date they lodged with the Commissioners a formal protest against their holding any further investigation of any claims in connection with the Carnatic Debt.

While the Government were considering these papers, evidence that the party headed by Abbott, Roebuck and Parry represented only a section of the mercantile community was supplied by a letter which was addressed to the Bengal Commissioners on the 18th January, 1809. This letter was signed by most of the leading firms in Madras: Lautour & Co. (which afterwards became Arbuthnot & Co.), Binny and Dennison, Colt, Hart and Weston, Harington, Tulloh & Co., S. H. Greig, De Fries & Co., De Monte & Co., Moorat, De Mello, etc. It began by expressing regret that the Commissioners should of late have experienced so many difficulties in the execution of their "arduous and important duty." It assured the Commissioners that the writers had "perfect confidence" that the Commissioners would discharge with ability and integrity all the duties of their office. It ended by suggesting that early steps should be taken to eliminate the large number of false bonds which were in circulation. In effect, this letter represented a vote of confidence in the Bengal Commissioners from all the leading firms in Madras.

Such a manifestation had little effect, if any, on the intransigeant section, which, early in February, perpetrated a further attack on the Commissioners. On the 3rd February, Abbott, Parry and Maitland wrote demanding to be furnished with copies of all informations sworn before the Commissioners, as it was their intention to institute further prosecutions against those who had supported Roya Reddi Row. The Commissioners refused to grant the copies. On the 7th February, Messrs. Abbott, Parry and Maitland then gave them notice that unless the copies were granted, they would move in the Supreme Court next day for criminal information against the Commissioners themselves.

This final outrage forced the Government to take action. For months the duties imposed on the Commissioners by the Statute and the orders of the Governor-General in Council had been held up by this small knot of men. Unless the plan for the settlement of the Carnatic Debt was to be radically altered, it was necessary to put a stop to these manœuvres. Mr. Abbott and his party had openly declared that the three Statutory Commissioners were, in their opinion, unfit for duty, and they now threatened them with a criminal prosecution. The Commissioners were well within the facts in informing the Government that unless steps were taken to assist them, it would be utterly impracticable for them to proceed with their work.

On the 8th February the Government issued orders. Mr. Benjamin Roebuck, who combined trade and official position, and who was Paymaster-General and Master of the Mint as well as partner in the firm of Abbott, Roebuck and Maitland, was removed from his appointments at Madras and ordered to proceed without delay to Vizagapatam and to take charge of the Factory there. Mr. R. A. Maitland, the third partner in the firm of Abbott & Co., was removed from the office of Magistrate in the Presidency. Mr. Thomas Parry, against whom the Directors' orders for his return to England had never been enforced, was informed that he should now be prepared to embark at the earliest opportunity. By these measures the small clique which had paralyzed the work of the Bengal Commissioners was broken up and they were left free to continue their inquiries in peace.

The result justified the action of the Government. The Commissioners, no longer disturbed by criminal prosecutions and threats of criminal prosecutions, carried on their investigations successfully. Additional information threw fresh light on the character of Roya Reddi Row. Serious reason for suspecting his good faith came to light. It was discovered that he had been concerned in the making of false entries in the Nabob's accounts. Eventually the Commissioners came to the conclusion that the bond for 38,500 pagodas, which they had at first pronounced to be genuine, was itself a forgery. They reported accordingly to the Commissioners in London, and this, as well as other bonds propounded by Roya Reddi Row, was turned down. The man himself died suddenly in July 1810, his death being popularly ascribed to poison taken under the shock caused by the Commissioners' discovery of his real character.

His enemy, Paupiah, had died earlier, at the beginning of 1809. As might have been expected from his previous history, the bonds which he had circulated were also found to be bad. Of him, as well as Roya Reddi Row, it may well be said that they were

"Arcades ambo." But in fact many quite reputable firms and persons found that the bonds which they held were bad. Claims to more than £350,000 which had been put forward on behalf of Mr. Roebuck, one of the leaders in the attempt to obstruct the Commissioners, had to be withdrawn, as the bonds were found to be forged. In the same way, Mr. Thomas Parry's claim, derived from Paupiah, for £27,000, was disallowed on the ground that nothing was due. When the Commissioners concluded their inquiry, only 2½ millions had been decreed in favour of claimants out of over 30 millions put forward.

The Bengal Commissioners were deservedly discredited by the revelations regarding Roya Reddi Row, but their good faith was not involved, and as soon as they discovered their mistake they took steps to rectify it. Still less could the Government of Sir George Barlow be rightly held to be to blame for the errors of their subordinates. They had merely performed a necessary duty in giving the Bengal Commissioners support, and were not a party to any erroneous conclusions at which the Commissioners arrived. But at the time the disclosures regarding Roya Reddi Row were eagerly seized upon by the enemies of Sir George Barlow, and the utmost possible capital was made out of the Bengal Commissioners' errors of judgment.

APPENDIX C

THE CASE OF MR. R. SHERSON

THE monsoon of 1806 having failed, the Government of Fort St. George, then presided over by Lord William Bentinck, thought it their duty to ensure an adequate supply of grain in the city. They accordingly arranged for the importation from Bengal of considerable quantities of rice, which was stored in a large number of warehouses, from 100 to 150 in all, on the sea-face. It was proposed to retail the rice at moderate rates to the poorer classes of the population.

An operation of this kind involved the expenditure of large sums of money which would be gradually recouped by the sale of the rice. It also involved the maintenance of accounts, which would show the receipts, issues and balances of rice, and the receipts of cash for rice sold—altogether a large and complicated matter of accounts.

The work was at first placed under a Committee, known as the Grain Committee, which consisted of Mr. Mungo Dick, a Member of the Board of Trade, Mr. W. Balfour, Collector of Customs, Mr. J. Kenworthy, Garrison Storekeeper, Captain Marshall, Secretary to the Military Board, and Mr. Robert Sherson, Reporter on External Commerce. From 1st April, 1807, however, Mr. Sherson was placed in entire charge of the work, subject to the general control of the Grain Committee, and he was given an assistant, Mr. William Cooke, a junior member of the Civil Service. He had, of course, a native staff also, an accountant in each godown and a head accountant and a manager in his own office. As Mr. Sherson was not "conversant" with any vernacular language,[1] he used to communicate his orders through his "personal dubash." In every godown, vernacular accounts were maintained. These were each day brought up at the close of work to Mr. Sherson's office, where an English abstract was made and submitted daily, under Mr. Sherson's initials, to the Grain Committee.

On the 10th and 11th December, 1807, Madras was visited by a violent cyclone which, in its ravages, unroofed and damaged several of the godowns where the rice was stored.

On the next day, 12th December, Mr. Mungo Dick, accompanied by Messrs. Sherson and Cooke, inspected the damaged godowns, five in number, to see what loss had been caused by the storm or by pilferers who might have taken advantage of the damage to the buildings to get in and steal grain. Mr. Dick came to the conclusion that the loss of grain, though appreciable, was not very great.

On the 19th December, Mr. Sherson sent to the Committee a detailed statement purporting to show the amount of grain lost by the cyclone. Although he submitted this statement with a letter signed by

[1] India Office Records: Home, Miscellaneous, Vol. 691, p. 624.

himself, he did not place his signature on the enclosure. The statement showed that out of about 20,700 bags of grain in the damaged godowns, 7500 bags,[1] or more than one-third, had been destroyed.

Mr. Mungo Dick received this statement on the 19th, and he at once proceeded, the same afternoon, in company with Mr. Sherson and Mr. Cooke, to inspect once more the damaged godowns. Mr. Dick made some rough calculations, measuring the floor space with his feet, and as a result, he declared that the loss was nothing like the 7500 bags shown in the statement and did not really exceed 1000 bags. He added that the statement must be false and that the native subordinates had falsified the figures. Mr. Sherson hotly controverted these remarks and contended that the statement was correct and that his subordinates were honest. The two chief subordinates were sent for, but both were absent, having, it was said, gone to get their food. One never returned and apparently absconded from Madras; the other reappeared some hours later. On being called on to produce the original vernacular vouchers (written on cadjans or dried strips of cocoanut leaves) on which the statement of the 19th December was based, this man said that all the vouchers up to the beginning of November had been destroyed. Mr. Dick then caused all the vouchers that could be found to be collected, and had them placed in a large chest in his presence. The chest was then locked and sealed by

[1] A bag of grain in Southern India would generally contain about 160 lbs.

Mr. Dick. Next day, 20th December, he made a report to the Government of the results of his inspection.

On the 21st December, as the Manager and Shroff were absent, Mr. Sherson broke open their desks, on the ground that these people had been in charge of his private cash and that he did not wish his private affairs to come before the Grain Committee. On the same date, Mr. Sherson, in a written note, informed the Committee that he now found that some of the bags of grain had been removed from the damaged godowns to other godowns, and that therefore the deficiency might be less than had been exhibited in the statement which he had sent in on 19th December.

Between the 19th and 24th December a further inquiry was held by the Grain Committee, who submitted to Government on the 24th inst. a report on the results.

Government then directed a further examination of the vernacular vouchers to be made by a fresh committee. When the chest, in which the vernacular vouchers had been locked up, came to be examined, it was found that the seals which had been placed on it by Mr. Dick on the 19th December were no longer intact.

On the 30th December, 1807, Mr. Sherson, who had taken no part in the Grain Committee's investigations, addressed a letter to Sir George Barlow, who had just arrived, demanding either that he should be entirely relieved of all responsibility for the grain in the godowns, the accounts and so on, or that he should be placed in undivided control, and be allowed to employ such subordinates as he might himself select, without any interference on the part of the Grain Committee or anyone else.

Meantime the Committee which had been appointed to examine the vernacular vouchers continued its investigations, and submitted a report to Government on the 26th January, 1808. With this report they sent a statement comparing the receipts from sale of rice during the first nineteen days of December as entered in the vernacular accounts with the same receipts as reported to the Grain Committee by Mr. Sherson. This statement showed that the sale receipts had been seriously understated in the statements submitted by Mr. Sherson, the short-entry amounting to over 8000 pagodas, or about £2800, in the nineteen days to which the statement related.

On the 29th January, Mr. Sherson wrote to the Government disclaiming any personal liability for any deficiency in the rice or the accounts and expressing a wish to go to England.

The Government took the opinion of the Advocate-General on the facts of the case as thus far disclosed, and as he advised that there was a good case against Mr. Sherson, they removed him in February 1808 from all his offices, and subsequently suspended him from the Service.

In the following June Mr. Sherson asked the Government to have his accounts audited by the civil auditor. The Government accordingly ordered the civil auditor, Mr. Smith, to make an audit. Disputes then arose between the Grain Committee and the civil auditor as to what accounts the audit was to cover, Mr. Smith declining to go into the question of the discrepancies between the vernacular accounts, which were, of course, the original basis of all the accounting, and the English accounts. On the 1st October the Government wrote to the civil auditor, countermanding their direction to him to make an audit, but on the 3rd October, Mr. Smith reported that his audit was already completed and at the disposal of Government. According to that audit there was no deficiency whatever in the grain accounts.

On the 25th October, 1808, Mr. Sherson left Madras and proceeded to England.

The first conclusion which emerges from the admitted facts of the case is that Mr. Sherson was guilty of gross negligence. On the 19th December he sent in a statement showing a loss of 7500 bags, which he afterwards admitted was entirely incorrect. It was subsequently pleaded on his behalf that as he did not sign the statement he could not be held responsible for it, and that the statement must be regarded merely as an estimate and not as a regular account. In reply to these pleas it was pointed out that the statement purported, not to be merely a rough estimate, but a minute and particular account, and that as Mr. Sherson sent it to the Grain Committee, he had clearly adopted it and was responsible for it. There can be no room for doubt that on the undisputed facts here proved Mr. Sherson was guilty of negligently furnishing an incorrect return, which incidentally was so drawn up as to cause heavy loss to the Company.

In addition to the misleading and incorrect statement of the 19th December, 1807, there was also clear evidence in the statement of monies received between the 1st and 19th December, that Mr. Sherson had also furnished day by day incorrect and misleading returns of the cash received in his office. No clearer case of negligence of the grossest kind could well be imagined.

Whether Mr. Sherson's action throughout all these proceedings was due to fraud on his part, or whether he merely signed and sent on without proper scrutiny the false statements prepared and placed before him by his subordinates, cannot now be ascertained. His conduct in attempting at first to defend the honesty of his subordinates, and in later breaking open their desks in order to secure access to their papers, thus giving him an opportunity of removing anything likely to incriminate himself, his refusal to take any part in unravelling the frauds which had gone on in his office, and his generally obstructive attitude towards the investigations made by the Grain Committee, all seem indicative of complicity in fraud. But however this may be, it is difficult to see what the Government could do but suspend such an officer; and the fact that Mr. William Petrie supported and countenanced Mr. Sherson and opposed the disciplinary measures taken against him by Sir George Barlow's Government throws a strong light on Mr. Petrie's own *bona fides*.

In July 1809 a "bill" for fraud was filed by the Government on the equity side of the Supreme Court against Mr. Sherson and his four chief Indian subordinates. Three out of the four Indians absconded. The reply of the fourth was filed in July 1812. Mr. Sherson was examined on commission in England in 1811. The case came on for hearing in March 1814 and the Company's bill was dismissed, but with permission to proceed afresh against Mr. Sherson on the principle of official responsibility.

In the year 1815, after Sir George Barlow had been recalled and all his official actions reversed, Mr. Sherson was reinstated in the Service and was voted by the Court of Directors a sum of 16,000 pagodas as compensation for his suspension. But this action was merely due to the change in the political atmosphere of Leadenhall Street, and can hardly be supposed to have any bearing on the question of Mr. Sherson's guilt or innocence of the charges brought against him.

APPENDIX D

LETTERS FROM SIR EDWARD PELLEW AND GENERAL MACDOWALL

(1) *From Sir Edward Pellew* [1] *to Sir George Barlow.*

Pte. de Galle,
14th *Feby*, 1809.

(Private.)

MY DEAR SIR GEORGE,

We have received the report of the Convoy ships leaving Colombo this morning, and we are now weighing to meet them. Last night an America Ship from Madras anchored here. She brought Colonel Capper, who, I find, landed instantly in great haste to seek General Macdowall. On my sending for the Master this morning, I learn from him that the Colonel landed with the Supra Cargo and have not been seen since. He stated, altho' incorrectly, that he heard some displeasure of your Government had caused the Colonel's resignation of his office or that you had suspended him—why he could not tell. But he believed signal guns had been fired from Madras to bring back the General and Convoy, but that failing

1. Sir Edward Pellew, Bart., Admiral of the Blue, afterwards Lord Exmouth, had been for several years Admiral on the East Indian Station, and his son, Captain Pownall Pellew, R.N., had married Eliza, eldest daughter of Sir George Barlow,

in effect, a dispatch boat had been pushed thro' the strait of Manaar to Colombo to General Macdowall. He also states the Deputy-Adjutant-General to have been removed about some orders issued by that officer, after the General's departure, to the Army. I am sorry to depart without knowing what this story is, but I shall get at it long before we reach Home and shall take care it is not related to the discredit of your Government.

In Confidence I told you some petty intrigues have been going on with the General and Mr. P . . . ie[1] before I left you. I suspect there has been some combination of arrangements brought about by all this late arrondisement[2] amidst the feasting of the Cantonments, on which you are no doubt on guard and well informed, and I believe the Heads of all *the Generals are laid together at Colombo at this instant.* I believe you know enough of Maitland of yourself. If not, I have had him on *Service* in my Cabin for six months. For the first he has no stamina when wanted, but is the most diabolical intriguer, sticking at nothing to obtain his ends, that ever was hatched from that democratic stock.[3]

Take my farewell good wishes for your health and

1 Mr. P . . ie. This is Mr. William Petrie, Member of the Council of the Governor of Madras.

2 Apparently this is an allusion to Lieutenant-General Macdowall's farewell tour to the military stations in Madras.

3 General Sir Thomas Maitland, Commander-in-Chief of Ceylon, was the younger brother, the eighth, of Lord Lauderdale, whose appointment as Governor-General was resisted on account of his republican principles.

happyness and offer them to Lady B. Let me beg you to believe, my dear Sir George, that you have a true and faithfull friend in your attached Servant,

ED. PELLEW.

P.S.—You will find at last that the loss [of the Ba][1]zar fund is the real cause of [the] [1] discontent and that is kept [up by][1] officers of every rank and description from Chief to drummer. Any other losses by better management of bullocks, tents, etc. will of course increase the heart burnings. You will get through it all with credit, I am sure and be well supported at Home.

Family all well.

Ships to weigh at Sunset.

(2) *From Admiral Sir Edwd. Pellew to Sir George Barlow.*

"Culloden," off Pointe de Galle,
15th February 1809, 4 *p.m.*

MY DEAR SIR GEORGE,

We are now joining the Colombo ships and a Schooner, apparently a Company's Cruizer, is following. I have no doubt of her being charged with the Bombay Dispatches and probably with the latest news from Cochin, Quilon, etc., which I shall of course take a good view of and give full explanations on my arrival. I have no doubt of your being able to adjust and settle all this affair before the rains are set in,

1 MS. injured.

notwithstanding all the difficulties you have to meet by the clamorous opposition at Madras, part of which I have now got hold of. Petrie, I hear, is minuting and in opposition. I believe you will do right to guard against old Roebuck,[1] who, I firmly believe, is not sound at bottom. You have a high opinion of lankey G—l.[2] I know Lord W.[3] detected him of great duplicity of conduct on several occasions. Colonel Capper has not been near me and Captain MacPherson only for a few moments, so that I have heard nothing from him, but I had a great deal from the American Supracargo, and among other statements he said, had the recall of the Convoy succeeded and the General been relanded under suspension, the Army were ripe for any measures,—so much for exaggeration by flying reports—you would have been lucky to have kept your seat and we might have met in England much sooner than you had any expectation of when we parted.

Psyche and *Piedmontaise*[4] are now together; *Diadaigneuse* expected here every minute, shall take *the Desvaynes* from Galle and proceed to Quilon, where

[1] "Old Roebuck" is Benjamin Roebuck, a servant of the Company who was also a partner of Mr. William Abbott. See Appendix A, p. 153 and Appendix B, passim.

[2] "Lankey G—l." Possibly this refers to Joseph Greenhill, a senior Civil servant, who was Paymaster and Garrison Storekeeper at Madras at this time. He died at Madras 18th June, 1812.

[3] "Lord W." is presumably Lord William Bentinck, who had preceded Sir George Barlow in the Governorship of Madras.

[4] *Psyche*, *Piedmontaise* and *La Dedaigneuse* were ships of the East India Squadron.

her investment of Ham and Cheese may be in a great request, and should Malcolm's force be ordered down, they will of course be attended by one or two of the Frigates at Bombay, so that you may be easy from *without*, and as we know two out of the three French Frigates are over to the Eastward, there is only one to approach, which I think they will not risque, nor has De Caen any force to send them if they ever made any demand on him to that effect. God Bless you.

We have just joined and Macdowall sent me the enclosed, which I send as they are. I have not seen him as it is dark. God Bless you, my dear Sir, ever yours,

ED. PELLEW.

Enclosure (1).

At Sea—15th February.

MY DEAR SIR,

I send you two letters, one from James Balfour, the other from Baker.

You will have heard of the proceedings against me at Madras, which have abundantly vexed and distressed me.

I have nothing official on the subject, and merely a copy of a very violent order of Government reflecting on my conduct and removing me from the Command, and after I had in fact sailed from the country.

I am very comfortable on board the *Lady Jane Dundas*.

I hope Captain and Mrs. Pellew and all your party are well.

Believe me with great esteem,

Your very faithful servant,

HAY MACDOWALL.

Enclosure (2).

MY DEAR SIR,

Excuse pencil. Your Letter tells me you wished to see me on board, but I am not very well and have rather laid *low* since I accidentally heard of the extraordinary conduct of the Madras Government. During the voyage will take an opportunity of stating the circumstances to you.

Your kind offer of accommodation I would with great gratitude accept, but I am quite snug and comfortable here. I beg to offer you my sincere acknowledgments.

Capper and Boles have been suspended the service *for obeying my orders.* I thought it necessary to reprimand Col. Munro and they issued my orders.

I will not add more at present, but trust that when the circumstances are made known to you, you will allow of the necessity on my part of not compromising the honor of the profession or the situation I held.

General Baillie came on board last night. Colonel and Mrs. Orr are quite well and all beg to present their best regards to you.

Most faithfully yours,

HAY MACDOWALL.

His Excellency.
Sir Ed. Pellew.

I find by your note that Captain Cochrane is on board the *Culloden.* Have the kindness to hand him the accompanying.—H. M.

(3) *Sir Edward Pellew to Sir George Barlow.*

"*Culloden,*" *Table Bay,*
14th April, 1809.

MY DEAR SIR GEORGE,

You will be glad to hear that we have escaped with our Convoy from the effects of a most violent gale of wind (I may indeed call it, rather, a Hurricane) by which we were assailed on the 14th, 15th and 16th of March in Lat. 23.30 S., Long. 61.00. A total separation took place and every body shifted for themselves, looking only to their own preservation, and more or less every ship suffered. The *Culloden* did not escape without great injury and loss; the particulars I have no doubt Eliza will convey to Lady Barlow. She had six men for one whole night bailing the water from under her bed. She did not, however, betray any feminine weakness and on the contrary was very heroic. The *Terpsichore* had a very narrow escape, blown down on her broadside for several hours. We are now in a tollerable state and had not the old *Culloden* been in good condition, she must have gone down; in fact, had it continued six hours longer with the same violence I believe she would have closed all our accounts in this life. We sail to-day patched up. Eight sail have gone on by my signal. The four Absentees are, I consider, gone on also to St. Helena,[1] which was the second rendezvous.

[1] The four "Absentees" or missing ships were never heard of again, and were lost, with all on board, including General Macdowall and Colonel Capper, in the hurricane of the 14th—16th March.

They were the best sailors, and Macdowall wished much to avoid the Cape: the reason you may conjecture: I believe he felt hurt to be shown to so large a military force as is here, under suspension. I do not think he had adverted to such a measure as coming within the reach of your ideas, or that it could have been resorted to. Our weather was such that I had scarce time to see him on any day but one, when we had considerable conversation on the subject, and I am quite satisfied he feels considerably and greatly regrets the circumstances and would give a great deal to retrace the ground he so imprudently and inconsiderately travelled out of his way to attain. We shall meet at St. Helena, where our delay will be longer than I had hoped, most of the Convoy will have to unload there.

Eliza is quite well, cheerful and happy and I believe in a way to repair her loss on the voyage from Calcutta. Lord Caledon has shown her, and all of us, marked attention and hospitable kindness. Mrs. Cotton is become a gay young widow, much adored by Capt. Cochrane and adoring him. Whether it will end in matrimony, I will not venture to say, and as both are past the days of imprudence, I have not thought it proper to interfere. But in the general opinion, matters are in a fair train.

News we can send you none which you will not have had long before you can read this, and no man will venture an opinion on public events for fear subsequent information should give the lye to his former communications.

I do not now calculate upon reaching England before the end of July.

Adieu, my dear Sir George, and believe me ever with sincere regard,

Your faithfull friend,
ED. PELLEW.

P.S.—I send a copy of *the William Pitt*'s statement and a list of our absentees. I fear the *Nelson*, *Ceylon* and *Glory*, of the *Albion*'s Convoy are lost. No news of them here and the only chance seems to be Bencoolen or St. Helena. *Albion* was near gone.

Convoy 11th April.

With Flag.	Ships gone for St. Helena.	Absentees.[1]
St. Vincent.	Wm. Pitt.	Calcutta.
Hugh Inglis.		Bengal.
Indus.	Huddart.	Jane Dundas.
Terpischore.	Euphrates.	Jane D. Gordon.
	Sovereign.	
	Lord Eldon.	
	Northumberland.	
	Harriet.	
	Sir Wm. Bensley—seen the 11th off Cape. Passed on next morning for St. Helena.	

American under Convoy from Madras passed on the 12th.

(4) *Sir Edward Pellew to Sir George Barlow.*

"*Culloden*," *St. Helena*,
8th May, 1809.

MY DEAR SIR GEORGE,

You will easily conceive my surprize on the

[1] See note on page 189.

appearance of Buchan and Dick[1] in the *Lushington* with your dispatches. I rejoyce however that you have adopted this wise measure, which I had very often thought (of) on my voyage, knowing what a nest of *malcontents* were in my convoy. My former letters will have told you Capper had joined the party and Macdowall had spared him half his Cabin. Buchan will, of course, write you at large from hence and give you his reasons for taking advantage of our protection, which plan, I think, will meet your wishes. The delay can only be 8 to 10 days, and by the papers the Channel is full of Privateers. Had not the other party lost ground by their separation (the four missing ships), having most probably gone into Simon's Bay to repair any damages, they sustained in the very violent gale we all suffered by, I should have urged dispatch. We move off for England to-morrow, as the *Russian* is here and will wait for the China ships, taking our four, should they arrive. This will give us a good month the start of Macdowall and prepare every subject for the consideration of the Directors.

You will remember my saying to you one day that I had not the favourable opinion of that *Body*. If you will look in the *Morning Chronicle*, you will be satisfied that I was right in my conjecture. I send you extracted the speech of Mr. Parry and Grant[2] at

[1] Mr. George Buchan was Chief Secretary to the Government of Madras, and was sent home by Sir George Barlow to represent personally the state of affairs in Madras. Mr. Mungo Dick was a member of the Board of Trade and had taken a prominent part in Mr. Sherson's case (see Appendix C).

[2] Mr. Edward Parry and Mr. Charles Grant were chairmen of the Court of Directors of the East India Company.

the Quarterly Meeting. That I was not recalled you know; however, as others may say so, I cover you copies of Lord Mulgrave's two last letters, that you may have the proof in your possession. Some explanation must of course follow with Mr. Parry on my arrival. The nature of this must be governed by the advice of my friends, as I shall do nothing rashly. The Chairman should certainly have informed himself better before he made so bold and unfounded an attack on the reputation of an officer of whom the Court cannot, in my opinion, complain of deficiency of attention to their interest.

I have read over very attentively all the papers you were good enough to permit Buchan to shew me, and from the very commencement the intention of the General to make common cause with *his Army* for his appointment to Council is evident, and in return, as their *Representative*, he, I conclude, promised to support their pretensions to remuneration and give his sanction to their helping themselves, if your Government refused complyance to their demands. That you have, by your firmness and moderation, broke down a chain formed for overturning your Government, there can be no doubt, and I trust you have persevered in sending Mr. Roe(buck) to Vizagapatam and Mr. Parry [1] over the surf. They are incendiaries of the first class, upheld and protected by Mr. P—e,[2] some of whose intrigues I once mentioned

[1] This is Mr. Thomas Parry, regarding whom see Appendix B.

[2] Mr. P—e is Mr. William Petrie, Member of the Council of the Governor of Madras.

to you. I wish I had not mentioned to you my young countryman in such warm terms. I fear Sir Henry[1] has infused the poison of insubordination strongly in him. His family have all strong republican principles, and a trip up the Country to a subordinate situation may be well applied for rooting out the bad effects of Sir Henry's doctrines.

You will perceive by my language that my communications with Buchan and Dick have been very unreserved. They are your firm friends, and Mr. P—e your confirmed enemy. He has contrived to overturn two Governments already; this was his aim and object now towards you; he deserves no mercy from you and I hope you will not spare him.

I shall take the best care of *Lushington* and push her forward whenever it is safe. I am not sure but I shall land Buchan and Dick in *Culloden* at Plymouth, from whence B. can run to Town in 30 hours. Dick and family can join my party for a slower journey. Pownell and Eliza, I believe, are writing. She is well and, thank God, happy and in a fair way to repair her former loss. We have found no chits from Lady B. or lazy Charlotte. Present me most sincerely and affectionately to them, and believe me ever, My Dear Sir George, your faithfully attached and affectionate friend,

ED. PELLEW.

P.S.—I rejoiced to hear the Travancore affair was

[1] Sir Henry is doubtless Sir Henry Gwillim, of whom an account is given in Appendix A.

upset.[1] I know great weight was given to that history by the Party and much aggravation. The wisdom of Buchan's going Home grows every moment more striking and necessary. I have written in great haste, which you will perceive. Pray excuse errors.

Absent Ships :—*Bengal*, *Calcutta*, *Lady Jane Dundas*, *Duchess of Gordon*.

[1] " The Travancore affair " probably refers to the intrigues set on foot by the Diwan of Travancore, and " the Party " is presumably the body of opponents of Government in Madras, which included Sir Henry Gwillim, Mr. Roebuck, Mr. Abbott, Mr. Thomas Parry and Mr. Marsh. This opposition party had been strenuously opposed to British intervention in Travancore.

APPENDIX E

SIR JOHN MALCOLM AND THE MADRAS MUTINY

In 1812 there was published in London a small work by Lieutenant-Colonel Malcolm (afterwards Sir John Malcolm) entitled *Observations on the Disturbances in the Madras Army*, 1809. It took the form of a strong attack on the policy of Sir George Barlow and the Madras Government, and as the work of an officer of known experience and ability, who had been an eye-witness of many of the events, it had considerable influence. It is a matter of some interest, therefore, to consider how far Malcolm was an impartial observer of the events he described.

Sir John Kaye, in his *Lives of Indian Officers*, has rightly pointed out how fundamentally Barlow and Malcolm were opposed in temperament. While both were admirable in their way, he says, they seemed to have been sent into the world to war with one another. Malcolm, big, breezy and rather boisterous, could have little sympathy for Barlow's caution and reserve. Malcolm, moreover, had taken up an attitude of strong opposition to the policy of pacification in Northern India which Lord Cornwallis initiated and Sir George Barlow carried out. It might, therefore, not be unlikely that he would be hostile to Barlow's policy in Madras.

An examination of Malcolm's letters lends strong

support to this view. As early as April 1809, before affairs in Madras had reached a crisis, we find Malcolm writing a series of letters which seem to have had for their main object the dissemination of suspicion of Barlow's proceedings. To Lord Minto, Lieutenant-Colonel Malcolm was suitably circumspect. He did not go much beyond saying that Sir George Barlow was intensely unpopular. "I know," he wrote, "that there is a personal irritation against him which exceeds all bounds, however unjust and indefensible." In this letter he is merely conveying guarded information to the Governor-General, to whom he suggests that it would be a wise precaution if he were to visit Madras.

On the same day Lieutenant-Colonel Malcolm, who was a most industrious letter-writer and who seems to have kept copies of all he wrote, sent a letter also to Lord Wellesley in England. In this he was a good deal more outspoken. "The degree of personal dislike which all ranks and classes have of him," he wrote, "is not to be described. This may be, and I dare say is, very indefensible, but it exists and cannot be changed." It will be observed that Malcolm here asserts that Barlow's unpopularity extended to "all ranks and classes." He does not allow that there existed any section of society or of officials which supported Sir George Barlow. The latter is represented as universally detested. Then the writer goes on: "I am quite satisfied of the purity and rectitude of Sir George Barlow's character. The public never had a more zealous or a more laborious servant, he is devoted to his duty and has no enjoyment beyond that of performing it. But his system is cold and inflexible, and proceeds on its course without the slightest attention to the feelings of those on whom it is to operate, and the present distracted state of affairs at Madras is, I fear, a comment, and a melancholy one, upon the result of such a system." It is perfectly clear from these words that, as early as the 18th April, Malcolm was definitely hostile to Sir George Barlow. An officer who could write in these terms was already an enemy, however much he might profess his belief in the "purity and rectitude" of Sir George Barlow's character.

But the batch of letters which Malcolm sent out at this moment is not yet complete. It also included one to the ex-Governor-General's brother, Sir Arthur Wellesley, the future Duke of Wellington, and already a person of importance and influence. To him Malcolm's attack on Barlow is even more damaging. "You know Sir George Barlow," he wrote. "He is a highly respectable public servant. His principles of action are all right and correct, but his measures are often ill-timed and consequently unfortunate. He generally leaves altogether out of the question that which would engage the chief attention of an abler ruler—men's minds; and though his cold system appears excellent in an abstract and general view, it often proves mischievous in its operation. He has another great fault which looks so like an excellence at first sight as to deceive most, he is perfectly inflexible with regard to everything that he deems a principle or rule. Now this is good on most occasions, but on some it is the height of folly." The picture thus drawn is of a man of mechanical mind, totally without sympathy or imagination, who, under the impulse of abstract ideas or preconceived principles, will steer the ship straight on the rocks, though any intelligent onlooker (such as Lieutenant-Colonel Malcolm) can see the danger.

It is not surprising that Lieutenant-Colonel Malcolm's visit to Masulipatam failed, for obviously he was entirely out of sympathy with the Government which he was nominally serving. He returned to Madras and watched with hardly disguised hostility the Government's action against the mutineers. When that action had proved successful and the mutiny was at an end, it became Malcolm's chief object to prove that the success was not in any way the result of Sir George Barlow's policy, but was due to other causes altogether. This appears from another series of letters which exists among the Wellesley MSS. in the British Museum.

One of these is a letter addressed to Lord Minto on the 25th August, 1809.[1] In this, while maintaining a becoming reticence regarding his feelings towards Sir George Barlow, he is at pains to insinuate that the collapse of the mutiny was not due to the Governor's measures, all of which had made matters worse, but to the intervention of the Governor-General. The surrender of the rebellious officers is ascribed to the news of Lord Minto's approach and to the "dignified

[1] Wellesley MSS., Volume No. 13637.

but conciliatory" terms of the "admirable order which you issued on the 20th July." The Governor-General is invited to believe that it was he alone who saved the situation in Madras, and that without him Sir George Barlow's proceedings must have ended in ruin.

Three weeks later Malcolm found it desirable also to write his views to Lord Wellesley. In this letter, dated 14th September, we no longer hear anything about Lord Minto's "admirable order" of the 20th July. The letter is a detailed and undisguised attack on Sir George Barlow, ushered in by Malcolm's usual preliminary protestations of respect. He begins: "I entertain my usual respect for the public principles and public virtues of Sir George Barlow, but am satisfied that his total want of knowledge of mankind and his insensibility of character has occasioned more mischief to the interests of his country than could have been produced in the same period by either the most profligate or most foolish ruler. I can never wish to soften or palliate the guilt of the officers of this Establishment, but they acted under the influence of temporary insanity, and it was a great object and one worthy of a true statesman to have saved such a body from destruction. No such endeavour was made and they were permitted, and I may almost say aided, in the great act of suicide which they have committed. Sir George Barlow satisfies himself that he acts in all cases as your Lordship would have done. The body of his Proceedings may at times have (for he has a good memory) the same shape, but the soul is inevitably wanting, and it is that which commands success. His presumption on this head puts me mad. It is that of a copying machine pretending to the genius and skill of him by whom it was formed and used." [1]

Having thus suggested to Lord Wellesley the conception of Barlow as attempting vainly to steal the late Governor-General's thunder, Lieutenant-Colonel Malcolm went on: "That Sir George Barlow has managed to disgust and irritate my mind, as he has that of almost every other human being, I will not deny, and though I am conscious of not having acted contrary to any principle of public duty, I feel so much for the situation in which I have been placed upon this and former occasions in Hindostan, where his character and system were equally displayed and would have done equal mischief if they had not been successfully opposed, that millions would not tempt me to serve under him, and of this resolution I shall inform Lord Minto in the most unqualified manner. I have no intention of remaining in India one hour longer than I am obliged, and I hope for the sake of my country that Sir George Barlow will not remain long. When Mr. Buchanan, with ambitious zeal, lately disturbed India with his plans of propagating the Gospel, it was anxiously wished by many he should obtain the lawn in England. The desire is much more general to see Sir George Barlow clothed in ermine and doomed for life to smile acquiescence on the measures of the Minister of the day."

This passage was intended to convey to Lord

[1] Wellesley MSS., No. 13637.

Wellesley the expediency of Sir George Barlow's recall. Malcolm then goes on to speak of Lord Minto. "Lord Minto is, I believe, a real great man, at least on the questions on which I have seen his mind called forth, he has shown himself such; he has, however, a most difficult part to act at this moment; it is one full of embarrassment, and has probably been rendered more so by the former communications with Sir George Barlow, who, as he deceived himself, probably deceived Lord Minto from stage to stage of this unfortunate transaction and obtained assurances and acts of support and approbation that might have been withheld, had a clearer and juster view of the subject been before him; but still Lord Minto is an enlarged and wise man and he is an English statesman; he has not been taught in an office in India to issue orders and form schemes without casting one thought on their operation and effect on those under his rule."

This passage seems also to contain an adroit appeal to the vanity of the person to whom it was addressed, who also was "an English nobleman" not "taught in an office in India," like Sir George Barlow.

The whole of the letter was a skilfully conceived attempt to prejudice Lord Wellesley against his former assistant and successor. In order that it might not be wasted on a single reader, a copy was sent to Sir Arthur Wellesley. It is perhaps not surprising that Malcolm did not include this epistle in his *Observations on the Disturbances in the Madras Army*.

APPENDIX F

SELECTION OF INTERCEPTED AND OTHER LETTERS WRITTEN DURING THE MUTINY

(India Office Records: Home, Miscellaneous, Vols. 698 and 736.)

(1) From the Committee, Hyderabad Subsidiary Force, dated Hyderabad, 23rd June, 1809, to the Officers, European Regiment, Masulipatam (Vol. 698, p. 490).

(2) From the Officers, Masulipatam, dated 5th July, 1809, to Brigadier-General Malcolm (Vol. 698, p. 499).

(3) From Lieutenant-Colonel J. Doveton, dated Jaulna, 13th July, 1809, to Lieutenant-Colonel Malcolm (Vol. 736, No. 36).

(4) From the Officers at Seringapatam, dated 17th July, 1809, to the European Regiment, Masulipatam (Vol. 698, No. 473).

(5) From Lieutenant Hugh Scott, dated Vizagapatam, 19th July, 1809, to Lieutenant-Colonel Malcolm (Vol. 736, No. 37).

(6) From Lieutenant-Colonel Malcolm, dated Masulipatam, 20th July, 1809, to a Field Officer (Vol. 698, p. 458).

(7) From Lieutenant A. Johnstone, 6th Native

Cavalry, dated Chingleput, 20th July, 1809, to Cornet Russell of the same regiment (Vol. 698, p. 477).

(8) From the Bellary Committee, dated Bellary, 24th July, 1809, to Lieutenant Scott, 6th Native Cavalry, Trichinopoly (Vol. 698, p. 479).

(9) From Captain J. M. Coombs, 25th Regiment, Native Infantry, dated Chingleput, 26th July, 1809, to Hodgson (?) (Vol. 698, p. 559).

(10) From the Bangalore Committee, dated Bangalore, 28th July, 1809, to the Committee at Trichinopoly (Vol. 698, p. 469).

(11) From Captain A. McLeod, 8th Native Cavalry, dated Jaulna, 1st August, 1809, to Captain A. McLeod, 9th Native Infantry (Vol. 698, p. 505).

(12) From . . . dated Secunderabad, 12th August, 1809, to Hadley (?) (Vol. 698, p. 449).

(13) From the Seringapatam Committee, dated 12th August, 1809, to the Committee Hyderabad Subsidiary Force or the Masulipatam Force (Vol. 698, p. 427).

(14) From Lieutenant J. Turner, 15th Native Infantry, Seringapatam, to Lieutenant A. Turner, Pondicherry (date about 12th August, 1809) (Vol. 698, p. 429).

(15) From . . . dated Jaulna, 12th August, 1809, to Mr. George Stratton of the Civil Service (Vol. 698, p. 529).

(16) From Major Geo. Poignand, Madras Artillery, dated Jaulna, 12th August, 1809, to Captain

John Noble of the same Corps (Vol. 698, p. 516).

(17) From Captain A. H. D(avidson), 4th Native Cavalry, dated Jaulna, 13th August, 1809, to "James" at Arcot (Vol. 698, p. 522).

(18) From . . . dated Jaulna, 14th August, 1809, to Captain Patterson (Vol. 698, p. 547).

(19) From Colonel Barry Close, dated 15th August, 1809, to Lieutenant-Colonel Malcolm (Vol. 736, No. 40).

(20) From Major Neale, 1st Native Cavalry, dated Secunderabad, 16th August, 1809, to Lieutenant-Colonel Rumley, 5th Cavalry (Vol. 698, p. 451).

Enclosure. Copy of a Private Letter from Lieutenant-Colonel Malcolm to a Field Officer, dated Masulipatam, 20th July, 1809. (*See No.* 6, *supra.*)

(21) From Major George Poignand, Madras Artillery, dated Jaulna, 18th August, 1809, to Captain J. Noble of the same Corps (Vol. 698, p. 535).

(22) From . . . dated Bangalore, 18th August, 1809 (Vol. 698, p. 421).

(23) From Captain S. Macdowall, 18th Native Infantry, dated Hyderabad, 19th August, 1809, to Major Welsh, 3rd Native Infantry (Vol. 698, p. 464).

(24) From Lieutenant Baker, 8th Native Infantry, dated Malgotta, Mysore, 29th August, 1809, to his brother (Vol. 698, p. 440).

(25) From Lieutenant T. S. Williams, 15th Native

Infantry, dated Noymongol, on the Chittledrug Road, Mysore, 31st August, 1809, to Lieutenant John Crisp, 2nd Native Infantry (Vol. 698, p. 435).

No. 1.

Hyderabad, 23rd June, 1809

To the Officers of the Madras European Regiment, Masulipatam.

Gentlemen,

I had the honor of acknowledging your Letter of 11 June on 20th by Tappal addressed to Ensign Roy, since which I am desired to inform you that a regular Committee has been instituted here to investigate all correspondence and to act as the emergencies of the present state of affairs may dictate.

I am desired to make the following observations on your communications :—

On para. 4. We are at a loss to determine to what extent the words " no longer to obey the orders of those now exercising the Govt. of Madras " (are meant to go), whether the words are intended to embrace all orders whatever or only such as may affect the Army at large, Corps, or individuals who may hereafter fall under the displeasure of Government.

On para. 5. We do not consider that any charge can be preferred against Lieut.-Col. Leith, there being positively no ground for such that we know of. He may have been an enemy to the

> Army by advice given to the Govt. to their prejudice, but no thing specific that we have ever heard of has been alleged against him.

We have the honor to enclose a copy of an Address which we intend to forward by this Post to Sir George Barlow signed by all the Officers here and by the Jaulnah Force to the amount of 160 signatures. We beg leave to draw your attention to the words in the latter part of the paragraph, "and restoring to their situations all the Officers who have incurred the displeasure of Government." You will observe that the sweeping expression "all" must include the Officers of the European Regiment, so that, notwithstanding the necessary delay which has occurred to obtain the signatures of the Jaulna Force, the officers of the Madras European Regiment, who have lately fallen under the displeasure of the Madras Government, come under the spirit of the Address.

We are of opinion that if Sir George Barlow rescinds his order, including those respecting the Madras European Regiment, which is our firm intention shall be included, that every purpose will be answered and that Sir George Barlow's departure must necessarily follow such an act of humiliation.

On an attentive perusal of the events mentioned in your second paper, we declare that we cannot attach any criminality to the Officers of the Madras European Regiment and view the measures of the Officer Commanding the Army in Chief and which we may suppose must have had the sanction of the Madras

Government, as they relate to your Corps, to have been totally unmerited, cruel and derogatory.

We view with still greater emotions of surprize, alarm and indignation the *Threat* mentioned in your Letter as coming from the same source, that in the event of Lieutenant Spankie's refusal to accept the appointment of Quartermaster the Regiment should be reduced and the Officers placed on half pay.

It appears to us a most eligible step that Colonel Innes should be brought forward on charges preferred by you, for which the papers before us afford abundant matter, for forwarding unjust and unfounded reports to the Officer Commanding the Army in Chief which have caused the Regt. to be publicly and unmeritedly stigmatized.

We enclose a copy of a Paper sent to us via Jaulneah by which you will learn the sentiments of the Bombay Army who have thus liberally stept forward in support of that of the Coast. This paper we wish to be generally circulated through the different Provinces, and it is our intention to express to the Bombay Army our best acknowledgements for their spirited profession of their intentions towards our cause.

Though we have made some comments and objections on the papers you have sent us, yet be assured that we enter into the general spirit of their contents, and while we wait your reply, we, in the interim, give time to the Madras Government to profit by the cautionary Address we have before noticed and of which we enclose a copy.

Should the Threat already noticed be attempted to

be carried into execution, we declare that it is our determination to support you in resisting any orders of Government that may be issued for carrying such Threat into effect.

We are, Gentlemen, your obedient Servants,
The Committee of the Hyderabad Subsidiary Force.
73 Signatures deposited with the Secretary.

To the Officers of the Madras Army.

GENTLEMEN,

By a publication of an order in the Bombay Papers issued at your Presidency, we, with the greatest surprize and disgust, see the suspension of some of the best and most independent of your Officers, removed and suspended for coming forward in support of the just claims of your Army. Partaking of your feelings in the manner as we do, this is to assure you that there is not a dissenting voice regarding what part this Army will take in supporting you in the cause and to announce our readiness to join you in any manner that may be requisite to ensure your success and resist this tyrannical and oppressive conduct of the Governor of Madras and his advisers. Written by the Committee selected for the purpose of considering the Situation of the Bombay Army.

No. 2.

Masulipatam,
5th July, 1809.

To Brigadier-General Malcolm.

Sir,

The officers of the Garrison of Masulipatam have resolved upon mature deliberation to acquaint Brigadier-General Malcolm with the circumstances under which they stand. They conceive an explicit declaration of their Sentiments and intentions befitting the justice (of) the cause in which they are engaged and suitable to the high character of the person to whom this is addressed. The measures lately adopted by Government they look upon as oppressing and injurious to the rights of the Army. They conceive those officers lately suspended victims of their endeavours to support a just cause. They applaud their conduct and behold with mingled sensations of regret and indignation the result of their exertions. With feelings of equal regret and indignation have they witnessed the aspersion cast upon their reputation as a military body and seen the high character of the Coast Army impeached and branded in the Public Papers. They have therefore pledged themselves to their Brother Officers to support every measure tending to secure to the Army two grand points—abrogation of the Order of the 1st May and the attention of Government to their grievances. They will reluctantly resort to any extremity and it was with difficulty they were driven to this; but the most respectful petitions the Army could frame have been treated with the most contemptuous neglect and most valuable officers have been punished for stepping forward in defence of their just rights. This, Sir, is a candid avowal of the sentiments entertained by this Garrison and of the determination by which they are resolved to abide and as such they desire to be understood.

No. 3.

My dear Malcolm,

I was yesterday favoured with your Letter of the 4th July and which I was happy to see dated from Masulipatam, which I hailed as the most fortunate of all possible events in the present awful situation of affairs, as denoting the determination of Sir George Barlow to adopt the only measures now left to prevent utter ruin and confusion.

I wrote you a long reply to your former Letter, and which, as I despatched from here on the 16th June, I was in hopes you would have received on the 26th at Madras, but as you do not mention the receipt of it, it may perhaps have miscarried. I also wrote you a line on the 6th inst. enclosing copy of an Address from the officers here on Lord Minto after the receipt of the intelligence of the recent transactions.

. . . These I hope you will have received ere this reaches you. The horrid intelligence to which I alluded in that letter was the *solemn* determination of the officers of the Subsidiary Force at Secunderabad as well as at Jaulnah to march to the support of the officers at Masulipatam, should Government attempt to use force against them, and which intelligence I had then just been made acquainted with in a very extraordinary manner.

I immediately made known the contents of your Letter to me to all parties here and I am happy to say that it is a subject of universal congratulation. Indeed I think I may venture to prognosticate that if Sir George will only persevere in the plan he has *now* adopted, that his friends and supporters will daily increase and the wild and dreadful schemes of his opponents be completely frustrated. Remember that the whole Army have their eyes now fixed on *you* and affairs in your quarter! I am certain that you will and that the happiest results may be expected.

We have for some time since had the same report as you mention of the suspension of 15 officers of the Hyderabad and Jaulnah Force and to which had lately been added that of Col. Montresor's and my own deprivation of our commands. I have, however, from the good terms on which I am with all here, been able to prevail with them to suspend their belief of such reports, and from the same reason I may hope to continue to be of service to both parties "if severe measures are not again resorted to." But if they are, any attempt to save India will be vain! All is quiet here. Continue to send me regular accounts of what passes in your quarter, as it will be the means of counteracting reports of a different nature which will no doubt be attempted to be put in circulation and will therefore contribute most materially to the public welfare.

Ever your most sincerely,

Jaulna, 13*th July*, 1809. J. DOVETON.

No. 4.

Seringapatam,
17th July, 1809.

To any Officer,
Madras European Regiment, Masulipatam.

My dear T—,

I write you notes in various ways and directions as we are not sure of your receiving them regularly. We have received your papers of the 5th and 6th July, and all applaud the Garrison at Masulipatam for their spirited conduct. A general redress of grievances is thought necessary to be insisted upon. All are ready to obey your call. They are forming an Army at the Mount with an idea of frightening you, I suppose, but every man at it, with hardly an exception, is your sworn friend and will join you, should they move towards you. Our Force will make a cut through the Districts to support you. You may depend upon an unqualified support. The oftener we hear from you, if one line, the better.

Memo. Your papers have been duly circulated in every direction. Direct under a brown cover to Meerjaun Alabudeen, Sepoy Writer, or Vencariloiloo Havildar, G 2 Batt. Regiment. You know the Corps.

Copy of the Envelope:
To Captain (Bellary).

Dear,

Be so good as to enclose and forward safe to Cumbum and thence to Masulipatam by a private hand to Innacondah the enclosed. We take every means of letting them know our sentiments. Send it to an officer at Cumbum in whom confidence is to be placed and he will send it by a Sepoy to Innacondah.

No. 5.

Vizagapatam,
19th July.

To Lt. Colonel Malcolm.

My dear Colonel,

I have to return you many thanks for your last letter which reached me two days ago.

It would ill become me (nor indeed was it ever my intention) to enter the lists of controversy with you on this or any other political discussion. I merely took the liberty of expressing my feelings and sentiments to a friend from whom I have met with many kindnesses and for whom I shall ever retain that sense of personal gratitude and esteem which these kindnesses warrant and require.

The extremity to which the Army has at last had recourse is doubtless to be deplored, and, as you say, had Col. Taylor remained at Masulipatam, it never would have been brought to the push, at least a more feasible plea than that in which hostility has commenced would have been made use of. But having *commenced*, you must be sensible that firmness becomes the only salvation of the Army. It or Sir George Barlow (not the Government) must sink or swim, and I must still confess myself sufficiently the friend of the Army to hope that it may *swim*. Nay, I will confess to you further that even if I were convinced that I am wrong, I would not now desert the Cause which I have espoused or the principles which I have avowed, and I declare that if opposition to the Coast Army were to take place and I, as a Govt. Officer, were called upon to *act* against them, I would resign my appointment and live or die with my brother officers.

I will not enter further into the business at present. Several copies of your Extract to me I have distributed, conceiving it to be your intention, in which idea Colonels — and — agreed with me. But the sentiments it contains have been made public too late in the day and may now have an opposite effect.

. . . . . .

Believe me, my dear Colonel, yours sincerely,

HUGH SCOTT.

No. 6.

Masulipatam,
20 *July*, 1809.

Copy of a Private Lr. fr. Lt. Col. Malcolm to a Field Officer.

I have received your kind Letter of the 8th inst. but fear your hopes of my success will be disappointed. The voice of passion is alone heard and every man that speaks with temper and reason is condemned and calumniated.

The crisis, in fact, if not arrived, appears now near at hand, when every officer in the Company's service must determine whether he will maintain his allegiance to the Government he serves, to the King and to his Country, or decidedly throw it off, and assuredly there is no individual who claims a title to any spirit of independence who will (not) exercise his judgment upon a question which must so deeply involve all his future prospects of happiness. If ever there was a moment in which it was important for a man to look at those consequences which are likely to ensue from one step more in their course, it is the present, and it is assuredly worth while to pause for a moment and examine coolly the nature of our grievances and the length we are justified in going to obtain redress of them and the probable consequences to ourselves and to our country of throwing off our allegiance to the State. There were accounts by the last dispatches that the existance of grievances in this Army was already a topic of public discussion. General Macdowall and Colonel Capper have no doubt arrived before this in England and they would be soon followed by Colonel St. Leger and the other suspended officers. Is it not evident that all the aggrieved parties in England, the public records which must be transmitted, and the voluminous private correspondence which every ship since those transactions took place has carried home, that every one of the topics of complaint will be a subject of warm discussion, and will not the agitation they have created in the Army be brought fully forward, and have we not reason to conclude from all these circumstances that an early settlement of these questions will be made by those authorities by whom they must at all events be ultimately judged, unless this Country should prematurely throw off its allegiance and obedience to England? As far as we can judge from the past there appears reason to anticipate a fair and liberal dicision from the controlling authorities at home. They have hitherto certainly judged questions of this nature with great attention to both the feelings and interests of the Indian Army.

With this prospect can we be justified in resorting to such desperate extremes because we are discontented with the acts of a temporary local Government, and not only involving ourselves in ruin but injuring in the deepest manner our Country at a moment when it is the duty of every man who has a spark of patriotism in his breast to support her against the numerous and powerful enemies by whom she is assailed?

But we proceed, it is said, in the certainty that Government may see those evils and that it will give way in order to avoid them and that indeed it has no power, if it wished, to oppose our spirited and united demand of a full redress of grievances.

Let us examine these points. Government may see great evils in our resistance of its authority but may perceive still greater in yielding to the peremptory demands of an armed body confederated for the purpose of intimidating it into concession. It is the extreme of the pressure in cases of this nature which too often causes the resistance; and as to its power of opposing any attacks upon its authority, it is perhaps much greater than we at the moment calculated. There can be no doubt of the fidelity of all the King's Troops to Government. It has a large body, not less than 10,000 disciplined infantry, 4000 Horse and

16,000 Peons belonging to the Mysore Government, all perfectly at its devotion; and it will, whenever a rupture takes place, regain, thro' the influence of some of the old officers, many of the native battalions. It will raise more troops, it will be compelled to promote officers from King's Regiments, to give commissions to serjeants, to raise young men at once to rank and reward all those who leave brother officers before a certain date, after which those in arms against its authority will be proclaimed rebels, and other men, both Europeans and Natives, tempted to desert and betray them by every inducement and encouragement that can be offered. All the means of Government, whatever they are, will be organized and regulated, and with such it will probably triumph. But alas! triumph will be over its own strength and will be the destruction of those who are its support, and glory such as this must be ten times more mournful than the most signal defeat from a foreign enemy.

Let us view the other side. When men have once passed the Rubicon and commenced opposition to the Government, what will be their plans? They must be settled by distant and probably divided Committees, and every young officer would feel, in such situation of affairs, a right to examine the actions of his superiors, and could any man under such circumstances, when the chain of discipline was broken, rely on the order and fidelity of his troops? What could be offered to induce them to resist the temptations held out by the Government, and if they did not desert, would they be equal to encounter the Army of the State?

But say they were superior, that they were led to victory and our mad passions were gratified, at what pain and would they arrive (*sic*)? Could we expect our King and Country to receive us again into favour when our hands were red with the blood of British subjects that we had led and assisted the Natives of India to shed, and could we expect those Natives would allow a few officers to continue their rule over them after they had been taught to condemn the authority of and slaughter the soldiers of the British Government?

But it is stated that we have gone so far that to retreat would be to expose ourselves to shame and degradation. Gracious God! what an argument is this! Would men recollecting themselves on the verge of guilt and stopping under the action of loyal and patriotic motives in a cause to which they had been led by strong feelings of injury, be subjects of reproach or disgrace? Would it not raise their reputation higher than ever and entitle them to look for a redress of their grievances with proud confidence to that country to which they had so strongly proved their attachment? Could it fail of exciting feelings even in the local Government which must lead to those very conciliatory acts which it will be in vain to contemplate if sought with the bayonet?

This is the future which presents itself to my mind of the line now before us. I contemplate it with horror, and you may judge my present feelings when

I declare to God that, in the part I must take with those of my brother officers who are so deluded as to rush into an open warfare with the Government they serve and their Country, I shall, I am satisfied, be (more) happy if I shall be killed by the first ball that is fired in this horrid and unnatural conflict than if I had to see it terminated. I see no possible mode in which the impending evils can be averted but by the *action* of the good and loyal feelings of the majority of the officers of the Army, and of this action I do not yet despair. I must indeed to the last continue to hope that this noble spirit will show itself and save us from the gulph of destruction.

I am now busy with an enquiry into past proceedings at this place, with the report of which I shall proceed in a few days to Madras, and God grant that my efforts may be useful in averting the shocking calamities that are impending. At all events I shall have fulfilled my duty to my Brother-Officers, to Government, and to my Country, and that reflection will render every event a consolation during my existence.

No. 7.

Chingleput, 20th July, 1809.

MY DEAR RUSSELL,

Here I am thus far on my route to Madras, living with your Brother, but from the late extraordinary proceedings of Government (which I find he has given you an account of by yesterday's Tappall) do not intend to continue my journey. Another thing which induces me to turn back is a Letter that Captain Caldwell, who is here likewise, received this morning from Gordon, stating that he was in hopes that I would sign the Pledge and that I should, by doing so, be appointed to one of the Corps of Cavalry at the Mount. I understand all the officers of the Company's service will be called upon to sign it and in case of a refusal they will (as those of the 3rd and 7th) be sent away to some distant part of the country so as to have no communication with our Regiments. I certainly, for one, do not put my name down to the Test and I think I may venture to say that no officer of the 6th will, excepting one or two names I will not mention. I dare say you know who I mean.

Has neither said anything about my returning to the Corps? pray write and let me know. Direct your letters to Pondicherry, which place I shall return to without delay.

Should the purport of the expresses lately gone to Trichinopoly be to order our Regiment to the Mount, do not forget to put my Tent on Bullocks and bring it down with you.

Your brother has a remarkable fine Spaniel for you, and your being a sportsman, she will prove of great advantage to you. Adieu, believe me ever yours sincerely,

A. JOHNSTONE.

P.S.—Remember me kindly to all friends. Conway (is) Comm--- (of) one of the Regiments of Cavalry and Blacker the other. I am afraid that Babington will be kidnapped. I hope to God he will not sign. Do not forget to write me word if neither has thrown out any hints relative to my journey.

No. 8.

Bellary, 24*th July*, 1809.

To Lieutenant Scott, 6th Native Cavalry,
Trichinopoly.

SIR,

We have the pleasure to forward to you letters from Hyderabad received here by yesterday's Tappall. The measures of the different Committees at Jaulnah, Hyderabad and Masulipatam we are preparing to follow up here in the most decided manner, and in the meantime we circulate copies of this important communication. A copy of another Letter from an officer at Seringapatam to the Masulipatam Regiment we also enclose, the opportunity of its passing this way to its address enabling us to do it. Some days ago, we had the following pleasing intelligence from Bengal which it may be worth while to communicate, that the force at Muttra, King's and Company's, had entered into subscription for the officers who have been or may be suspended by the Madras Government for exerting themselves in the cause of the Coast Army. Do us the favour to acknowledge the receipt of this.

THE BELLARY COMMITTEE.

Enclosure :

"Your support to the common cause of the Army against the oppression of our present Governor is now required, as the blow has been struck here on the event of which and the final determination of our Brothers at Masulipatam depends the fate of the Coast Army. The 2 Batt. 10th Regiment having been ordered to move from hence, as was naturally supposed here, with a design to disunite this force and by disunion to weaken us and then seize upon and sacrifice our officers: this also being contrary to the resolutions we have entered into for mutual support in the defence of the rights of the Army and the redress of our grievances, we have (as the annexed copies of letters, the first public and the second private will show) resisted the order for the removal of the 2nd of the 10th. You are therefore most earnestly requested, as you value your rights as free men and officers, to assist us against Sir George Barlow by addressing Government immediately in a Letter declaratory of your approbation of the measures of our Committee, your determination to support us, and your resolution not to march at the order of Government, but as the cause of the Army may require. You are requested further to circulate this paper as much as possible."

No. 9.

MY DEAR HODGSON,

I have just heard from an officer of the 6th Regiment Cavalry passing through here of your correct and most honorable conduct and I cannot refrain from expressing to you what I feel on the occasion, the sentiments of approbation which every honest man must feel at such disinterested, generous conduct. Be assured, my dear H., whatever temporary inconvenience you may suffer will be amply compensated by the encreased regard and esteem which every good man will feel towards you. You are now one of the many good and virtuous men who have suffered misfortune rather than compromise their honor and integrity. Your example will be properly appreciated and I think you may be convinced that those who are really your friends not only applaud your conduct but would readily imitate your example. We shall yet see better times when honest men may hold those situations without discredit or disgrace. In this I cannot say so much as I wish, for the Tappal is very far from safe. I fear the game is quite lost owing to folly and want of consistency. The Northern Division has not been supported by the other Divisions in the way it expected and I see nothing but defeat and disgrace likely *now* to ensue. I thought very different three days ago, but want of support is the evil. I cannot with prudence say more in this and I have written merely to express what I felt on hearing this day of your resignation.

Believe me to be, my dear Hodgson, very faithfully yours,

J. M. Coombs.

Chingleput, *26th July*, 1809.

Address to me Camp at the Race Stand. Look at the Seal, for the Tappal is suspected.

No. 10.

Bangalore, 28*th July*, 1809.

To the Committee of Trichinopoly.

Gentlemen,

We have the honor to enclose a paper just received from Bellary.

We wrote to you on the 20th inst. informing you that the Garrison of Seringapatam had refused to permit the 19th or Company Artillery to move to Bangalore as ordered.

Since this no offensive moment on the part of the King's Troops has taken place.

Private letters from Madras urge the necessity of an address being sent to Sir George, conveying our undisguised sentiments and determination. Such a one has been signed and a copy sent to you yesterday. We only wait the signature of the rest of the Division to send it on to Madras, from whence the Address will be sent in accompanied by the signatures of the officers in the Centre Division.

Private letters also state that Sir George has had two conferences with .Colonel Rumley and Floyer, but the result has not transpired.

The Bangalore Committee.

We think you had better forward to Captain West the signatures of the officers at Trichinopoly to the address we forwarded to you without waiting for those of the rest of the Division.

No. 11.

Jaulna, 1st August, 1809.

To Capt. A. Macleod,
9th Regt. Native Infantry,

MY DEAR MAC,

I have just now had the pleasure of receiving your Letter of the 14th July and can attribute your ignorance of what has happened here only to the vigilance of that Government which has driven us all to a state so distressing to the feelings of every Briton. Your Letter was extremely satisfactory, as (tho' far from doubting the utmost support from any part of our Brother officers) Men who have gone to the lengths we have must feel happy that the cause in which they have engaged meets the universal approbation of all who have spirit to feel and resent the unjust attempts made to degrade us. I have only time to give you a few heads of intelligence, but you will have particulars tomorrow from a most excellent fellow of your own Corps who lives with us, T. D. Burnet, to whom the Secretary of our Committee will give copies of all essential papers that have been sent from this place.

The thanks we received in Orders roused us from the lethargy in which we must have appeared to the rest of the Army to have been buried, and we began with an Address to the Army which was followed up by one to the Governor signed by 180 officers, representing in strong terms how much he was deceived if he considered the discontents of the Army as only partial, and assuring him that rescinding his extreme acts of power and adopting conciliatory measures could alone allay the ferment created in the Army. This appears to have no effect, and the conduct pursued towards the European Regiment induced the whole Northern Division, knowing our sentiments, to bring the business to a crisis, so deposed Colonel Innes and Major Storey (19th) took the command of Masulipatam. We then informed Government of our determination to support the people at Masulipatam; also a declaration that any attempt to divide or weaken this Force would be considered incompatible with the resolution to which we bound ourselves to one another, consequently would be disregarded, so the Battalion of the 10th at Hyderabad was prevented from marching agreeably to the Government Orders, for Goa. The People at Hyderabad have requested part of us in advance to move towards them, but Meer Cawn is ready in our frontier to march in if we move back, so that the only mode in my opinion to bring Sir G. B., if not callous to every feeling of humanity or patriotism, to a sense of the necessity of the change of measures would be our declaring fully, and that without delay, as much as we have done, for nothing can prevent our moving, but your spirited exertions in the exterior (*sic*) while we are keeping off the general Foe who, I fear, has but too good information of what is going on. We had a Letter from the 3rd and 7th Native Cavalry this morning who assure us that tho' they are now on their march to Madras to join the Force forming at the Mount, they are ready to co-operate with us in any measure that may be deemed for the general benefit. I have not time to give you a word more, only hope that with perseverance you may make this out and give me the sentiments of your part of the World with as little delay as possible.

Believe me, my dear Alex, most sincerely yours,

A. McLeod
(of the 8th Regt.
Native Cavalry).

No. 12.

Secunderabad, 12 *August*, 1809.

My dear Hadley,

Things have turned out badly since I last wrote to you. We have heard that the troops in all quarters have signed the test: also left their corps. It is now near 3 weeks since we have heard from Jaulna, though they were ordered to join us. Proclamations have been issued to the Native Troops privately. The Subsidiary Force finding themselves completely deserted, or supposing it to be the case, yesterday signed the test and enclosed it in an address to Lord Minto; they had not the option like you of leaving the Corps or else they would have done it. I am getting much better and think I shall be able to march in about 3 weeks. We have brought our pigs to a fine market. In an Address to Lord Minto, we congratulate him on his arrival, regret much the state things are in, and give up all private animosity to the welfare of our Country, to convince him of which we have signed the Test and rely on his Lordship's generosity that the past may be consigned to oblivion and an Armistice (? Amnesty) granted the Army. God knows what will become of us. Times are bad. I begin to think the world is approaching to its end. At all events, I shall leave it with Credit. Remember me most kindly to all and believe me,

Yours most sincerely,

ROBT.

P.S.—Since writing the above we have just heard that Patullo of the Body Guard and Captain Frazer are both in close arrest on account of having refused to do what Sir George ordered them: that was written to their Brother Officers at Masulipatam, and let me know if you have left your Regiment or not—advice.

No. 13.

Seringapatam, 12 *August*, 1809.

To the Committee of the Hyderabad Subsidiary Force, or the Masulipatam Force.

The 1st Battn. 8th, 1st Battn. 15th, 2nd Battn. 15th, 2nd Batt. 19th Regiments and the Artillery are now in possession of this place. The two former Corps came in yesterday, after being assailed by all Purneah's Horse from the time they left Serah. When they got within 4 miles of this, they were charged by 2000 of Purniah's Horse and all the 25th Dragoons, the 59th

Marching directly against them. Resistance was in vain, they all threw down their Arms and made for the Fort. By this means they have joined us with the loss of Captain McIntosh of the 8th and Lieutenant Best: the former supposed to be taken and the latter died of fatigue; about 100 men killed and wounded. The 25th Dragoons have drawn the first blood, cruelly killing even little boys and men without arms. *Revenge, Revenge!* All the Masulipatam, Hyderabad and Jaulnah Forces ought to move by the shortest notice to this Station. We will never give up this place. We have 200 Artillery and can furnish everything for an immense field Train. We can then defy any force that can be brought against us. Our Men are all, in spite of this misfortune, in the highest spirit, ready for anything. The Treasure at Adoni and Anantapore ought to be seized, if possible. We expect that the whole of the Travancore force are concentrating for the purpose of joining us. The two Corps at Dindigul and Palamcottah will retire to Travancore on the approach of an European force. We earnestly entreat you will take this plan into your most serious consideration as the only means of saving us from certain destruction. We can hold out for two or three months but not longer, and you can expect nothing further from us than retaining this place. Last night, in retaliation for the infamous part the 25th Dragoons have acted, Guns and Mortars were placed to bear on their Camp, a cannonade of Shells and round commenced about 12 at night and lasted for two hours. Great execution was done. It is said 300 men were killed and wounded. They have been the Aggressors. We were driven to it.

THE SERINGAPATAM COMMITTEE.

No. 14.

To Lieutenant A. Turner,
Pondicherry.

MY DEAR ALEXANDER,

You will no doubt lament with me the measures we have been obliged to take against the Tyrant, but it is to be hoped the business will be settled without bloodshed, as there is nothing we more wish than to be upon good terms with the King's Troops. We some time ago took possession of this Garrison, where we have all the Artillery (as fine a train as any in the world) for any number of Troops, the 2nd Battn. 15th and 2nd Battn. 19th, all the Privates of which Corps have solemnly sworn to die with their Officers and never to be commanded by King's. We shall not be the first to fire a shot, but we are solemnly pledged, if attacked, to defend the place to the last extremity. Nothing can take it except famine, and I assure you we have grain sufficiently for 600 men for 6 months and pay for that time. The Northern Army by that time will settle the dispute, if Sir George is so mad as (to) go on with his measures; but Lord Minto will be round and I am sure he will settle it. The troops at the Mount from whom their Officers were taken, have sworn to return to them the first opportunity, or join the Company's Troops, when assembled, so that they will all go over to the Northern Army.

The Garn. have sworn to live and die with us and we shall all lay in an Embrazure before we surrender.

I think the Bengalees will go mad when they hear of the late measures—the Bombay Army have already taken an active part.

Yours ever,

J. TURNER.

I send this by Bangalore by a private *hand* as all Letters are stopped here.

No. 15.

Jaulna, 12*th August*, 1809.

MY DEAR STRATTON,

My long silence has, no doubt, appeared extraordinary to you, but when you reflect on the extreme solicitude and anxiety which we have suffered for the last three months on account of the crisis approaching, you will pardon my neglect. The Sword has been drawn. The Hydrabad Force have declared the present Government illegal and have solemnly disclaimed its orders. I shall now proceed to detail the affairs, which have lately occurred, as minutely as possible. Government assembled a considerable Force at the Mount composed partly of Europeans and Natives and organised them into two Brigades, one of Cavalry and one of Infantry. When they conceived the favourable opportunity had arrived for discovering the sentiments of the Officers of the Native Corps assembled at the Mount and Madras, they convened the Commandants of those Corps at the Presidency in the Fort, while those who were stationed at the Mount were directed to meet at Colonel Harris's Quarters. In consequence of this order, the officers repaired to the respective places, when a test was tendered to them couched, as I understand, to the following purport, that they should act according to the laws of their King and Country and obey implicitly all the orders of the Government of Fort St. George. This the Company's officers positively refused to take, as the evident tendency of the Oath was to obliged them to draw their swords against their brother-officers. A Guard of Europeans waited to seize them and they were sent off to three different Stations to the number of 120. Only six scoundrels accepted of the proffered Test; their names are known and I suspect that inevitable disgrace, infamy and perhaps more fatal consequences await their abject submission to such an unprincipled Government. This treacherous deed is worthy of the dark ages and can only be supported on principles since declared base in Europe and only practiced by those nations remarkable for their brutality or degeneracy of manners. When once that confidence is destroyed which naturally unites individuals to each other, the Government will endeavour in vain to convince the Army of their justice or desire of conciliation.

Colonel Close having been appointed to the command of the Subsidiary Force, it was the determination of the Officers composing that part of the Subsidiary Force situated at Hydrabad to prevent his assuming the dignity without he declared upon his honor his opinions in the most unequivocal manner and pledged himself to take no measures to the prejudice of the Army. On his arrival at the Resident's House, a deputation of field officers waited on him, requesting to know the powers with which Government had furnished him and if a General Amnesty to all the officers, especially to those of Masulipatam, formed a part of them. He replied that he possessed no authority of that nature, but showed them the test, upon which they stated that they should renounce his authority and pay no obedience to his Orders. In the meantime, Colonel Close, I suppose as he thought slipped privately out and pushed for the Cantonment, as he was acquainted with Orders directing the Troops to assemble that morning. Fortunately the two Field Officers suspected his intentions and followed him and by their superior local knowledge gained the Cantonment before him and beat to arms. On his arrival on the right of the line, he found the Corps there stationed in open column wheeled outwards for the purpose of flanking the remainder, as the 33rd Regiment of Foot were expected. He harangued the Men and said that he had fought and bled with them and told them their officers were leading them astray and acting illegally. Immediately the officer in front wheeled them into line and on his approaching nearer, ordered them to prime and load. Upon this he attempted to pass to their right, but the officer commanding the Artillery immediately drew up his guns to flank the 16th and a Company of Grenadiers were sent to seize Colonel Close. When he perceived the Grenadiers in the rear, he asked the officers for what purpose they came there. The reply was to secure his person. Upon this, it is said, he was completely thunderstruck and requested to be permitted to deliver up his sword to the Senior officer present and desired them to witness that he had conscientiously performed the Orders of the Supreme Government and resigned the command to Colonel Montresor. At the very period that Colonel Close was secured, the 33rd were marching down the right, and it was conjectured to be his intention to seize the Company's officers in the event of the Troops obeying his directions. If you wish to know the character Colonel Close might have been, read the letter of Junius addressed to the Duke of Bedford, commencing with the expressions "I shall now inform you what such a person as the Duke could do." Such a wretched, humiliating compliance with the orders of a tyrannical Government has for ever tarnished the character of Colonel Close in the eyes of the Army. That fame and reputation which has been the result of the most meritorious service during the period of between thirty or forty years' service is vanished like the fabric of a vision, and the most mortifying reflections on the steps he has taken must embitter his future days and perhaps bring his grey hairs with sorrow to the grave. If Colonel Close had acted that manly part which the Army naturally expected from a person of his distinguished zeal and abilities matters would never have come to this crisis, but he has suffered himself to be the tool of Government, and under the subterfuge of conscientiously obeying their orders, instigated the men to the most violent and destructive designs. Adieu, we march the day after to-morrow. God only knows what may be our fate, and if we are doomed to perish we shall perish the Martyrs of Liberty, and with our lives the British Empire in the East will be extinguished.

Your's ever.

No. 16.

Jaulna, 12*th August*, 1809.

MY DEAR NOBLE,

We have been in a terrible state of suspense for some time and I assure you my mind has been much agitated of late. We are 5 days without a Tappal and had, in consequence of information received from Hyderabad, every reason to suppose something was going on. The Hyderabad Committee had called upon us to send a detachment to them. They repeated this call and we waited upon Colonel D. and had a conference on the subject; however he still was of opinion that no part of this force should move till Government first declared hostilities, and then, as he had pledged himself all along, he would put himself at our head. This has now been put to the test. As I have just mentioned, we had been 5 days without a mail and the Colonel said, if we were 7, he should consider it was stopped by Government and act accordingly. However yesterday morning we were relieved of our extreme suspense by the arrival of 2 or 3 together and bringing your Letters of the 26th and 28th. They were received by me with a mixture of pain and pleasure. You tell me I have command of the Corps and, Noble, shall (?) head it to the last drop of blood in the cause. I immediately waited on the Colonel. He had received a letter from Lyne at Hyderabad giving an account of all that had passed there. I showed him yours; this was sufficient, the blow was struck from the right quarter and we march the day after tomorrow with the whole force, and Doveton, who is a noble fellow, at our head. If necessary, we shall be at Hyderabad in 15 days. You may suppose I am in great confusion and I have just now taken up my pen at 9 o'clock at night to finish my letter. I have so much to say I know not how to tell you all; this has been an awful day. The Colonel yesterday told us that he would sound the Native officers and would then parade all the Force and tell them plainly what was going on and what were his intentions. The conference he had with his confidential officers was favourable, and we all paraded this evening, when he addressed every Corps, and every man has declared he will stand by his officers. This measure in the present state of affairs necessarily had an effect on my mind which I need not describe to you. But I can only add in Doveton's last words to each corps, "our cause is a just one and God will support us." A Declaration to the Army and to the whole world has been drawn up and signed by all. A copy of this shall be sent you, but I know not even whether this will ever reach you. I shall address it to some Agent at Madras and hope to know soon where you are. I must tell you I addressed our men on Parade yesterday evening; I told them all that had passed and that you were removed from us. They will stand by us to the last and I trust, Noble, you will be with us again. You must not quit India till order is restored, and after that I will never remain in the Horse Artillery under anyone but yourself. The Officers with me all feel for your situation and beg to be affectionately remembered and to assure you of their unalterable attachment. Every man must now come forward to crush so infamous a Villain. It has been fully ascertained that the Native Officers here have been tampered with by letter for some time past for nothing more or less than to cut our throats. O Great God, I know no name too bad for him. I have seen some G.O. appointing the *Test Boys* to Corps, but thank heaven I have not yet seen Morrison's name. I cannot write to him till I know how he is acting and perhaps I may never write to him again, but I have too good an opinion of him to suppose he will take the wrong side. The only chance we have now to prevent all the evils which must follow is the arrival and interference of Lord Minto, and it is impossible to imagine he will support measures which will inevitably lose the country. We are in hopes of assembling in a very short time an Army of 30,000 men and it is not impossible that you will all join us. We move the day after tomorrow with the whole depot, which Blair has just brought us. We are to move out together, and the Colonel then intends pushing on with the Cavalry, H. Artillery and Flank Companies. Blair, although, as Staff, has hitherto kept back, enters into the cause with us as every man must do who has any sense of honor, and if our Natives remain staunch we will make Sir G. (knock?) under. You will receive accounts of the Hyderabad affair with Colonel Close, whose character is gone forever. I have not time to tell you all: you must be well aware what a state I am in. However I hope to conduct myself as I should do, and let me assure you, my dear Noble, of my sincere and affectionate wishes towards you. You shall hear from me again soon. I trust you will be able to make out this unconnected epistle, and I am not in a state to write on any other subject but the present unhappy one. With the affectionate remembrances of all your Officers believe me ever to be yours,

GEO. POIGNAND.

No. 17.

Camp at Jaulna, 13 *August*, 1809.

MY DEAR JAMES,

In consequence of the horrid and unprecedented state of affairs, I write these few lines to you to let you know that this Force marches to-morrow for Hyderabad. We have all heard with sentiments of the utmost indignation and concern of the late business at Madras. Colonel Doveton, our gallant and intrepid leader, paraded the troops yesterday evening. He explained to them every act of the Government, and asked them if they would stand by him and their Officers with their lives. The Horse and Foot Artillery, the Cavalry and Infantry assured him with repeated exclamations that they would stand to the last. The Hyderabad Force are, thank God, of the same opinion. We, therefore, my dear James, march in the highest spirits, trusting our just cause in the hands of the Almighty. I am sure you at Arcot and Counatore must be acquainted with this intelligence. Join us, my fine fellow. The colonel declares that the old 3rd and 7th will join him: our Sepoys say the same. Huzza! make my warmest regards to all friends and believe me ever yours most affectionately,

A. H. D.(AVIDSON).

Write to Mrs. Fullerton: tell her I am well and send her a copy of the Manifesto. I forgot to mention that our Men swore before God to stand by us. The enclosed is our Manifesto: circulate it everywhere.

No. 18.

Camp at Jaulnah, 14 *Aug.*, 1809.

MY DEAR PATTERSON,

It is some time since you and I have corresponded, but in the present unexampled and dreadful state of Public Affairs in this part of the Globe, I cannot refuse myself the pleasure of inclosing you a copy of the Declaration which, previous to our marching from our Port, the Officers of the Jaulnah Force have deemed it necessary to make to your Army, our own, to our Mother Country, and to the world at large, as a justification of our Proceedings. We march from this tomorrow and will with the utmost rapidity form a junction with the Hydrabad force, who, I fancy, are on their march to meet us. The immediate cause of this movement was the infamous conduct of Government towards the Company's officers at Madras, and the Mount, and their still more horrid conduct at Hydrabad, that of exciting the Native Troops to disobey their Officers. God be praised that they did not succeed, for if they had, the loss of the Country, the destruction of the Company's Officers, and even of a great part of your Army must, in my opinion, have been the inevitable consequences. May eternal infamy attend the Villain that formed such a hellish plan. I have now to acquaint you, that on the receipt of the above intelligence, Colonel Doveton made up his mind to the part he would act, and yesterday ordered his Line, consisting of the Horse Artillery, two Regiments of Cavalry, and three Battalions with a proportion of Foot Artillery to parade, and made them acquainted with every circumstance that has taken place. He then told them of his intention of marching the whole of his force to endeavour to settle the business and asked them if they were willing to march with him and their officers, and I glory in saying that the Line resounded with exclamations of their determination to stand by their officers to the last.

I trust that as this Detachment has heretofore shown the greatest moderation and has refrained from proceeding to extremities until the repeated insults of Government compelled us as men of honour and Britons to stand forth for our rights, that the Governor-General will appreciate our forbearance and consider our present demands as fair and just.

If Government should be so mad as to continue the system of oppression, they must order His Majesty's Troops to attack us, and if so, what would be the consequence? But no! I cannot for a moment suppose that the arbitrary mandate of a Tyrant would arm Briton against Briton, Friend against Friend and Brother against Brother. No! Patterson, I firmly believe that His Majesty's Troops, being convinced of the justice of our Cause, would not draw a trigger against us. After this unfortunate business is settled, I hope to have the pleasure of meeting you, as I can have no doubt but there will be a Mahratta war.

Colonel Walker's Detachment in Gazeret, I understand, has already had a battle with them and has met with considerable loss. They are in very great strength at present on the banks of the Nerbuddah, and I dare say will take advantage of our absence to plunder this part of the country. Meer Khan, the man who led General Smith such a dance, commands them.

I hope you will write me and let me know what

you think of the present strange state of affairs, and in the meantime believe me to be, my dear Patterson, yours very sincerely.

Make my best regards to Major Travers.

Private.

No. 19.

47 *Coss W. of Hyderabad,*
15th August, 1809.

MY DEAR MALCOLM,

Captain Sydenham sent me your Packet of the 4th inst. accompanied by your Letter to him of the same date.

When you departed for Masulipatam, you do not seem to have understood sufficiently the line of proceeding which Sir George Barlow had it in mind to pursue. This, I consider as extremely unfortunate, as it led you to propose a plan of proceeding to him which he was little inclined to adopt, and the result is a little soreness which is perhaps natural. You have made the only explanation that was possible to Sir George, viz: that you were not master of his intended line of proceeding, but it does not appear to me to follow that because you observed a conciliatory mode of conduct at Masulipatam, conceiving that you were acting all along according to the intentions and wishes of Govt., therefore, since that conduct failed of effect, you should not give into a coercive mode of action, as *that* only calculated at the present stage of affairs to save the public cause by restoring obedience and order. In the civil disputes in Ireland, Lord Cornwallis first endeavoured to conciliate the minds of the Malcontents, but finding that this plan failed, he coerced them with vigour and reduced them to submission.

Two points appear to me to be evident:—1st. That as the Malcontents on the Coast continue to hold out, they ought to be coerced, and 2nd. that Government is so powerful in means as to be able to coerce them. Although such are my opinions, I can easily make allowance for feelings that incline to a different direction and the powerful operation which they are capable of. They naturally enough seek relief by suggesting the plan of retiring. But however this may be, principles are stubborn. The common rule in time of civil dissention is "Look to your Country." Men, you know, are known by their objects and by occasions. The largest object before us is our country and the greatest occasion that can put us to a test is to be called on to save or guard it. I have mentioned this to Captain Sydenham. It could not have been pleasant to Govt. to bring forward the prescribed Declaration, but when menaced a Government must do something for its safety and, in respect to myself, I would rather command the necessity that compelled the adoption of the measure than find fault with the measure itself.

You will learn before this comes to hand that the Officers at Hyderabad have signed the prescribed Declaration, addressing a Letter to Lord Minto at the same time, of a nature that may be deemed perhaps not quite unexceptionable. The act of signing, however, does them great credit, and although his Lordship may be inclined to pass some strictures on their address, I doubt not but he will grant the pardon which they have solicited for themselves without allowing them to take any concern in obtaining pardon for others. Although they have signed the declaration at a late hour, still their example in signing when they did cannot fail to be highly useful, and on this ground his Lordship may be induced to grant their Address a favourable consideration. If the Officers at Hyderabad will, on being desired, attend at Col. Montresor's Quarters and sign the Declaration in the manner simply in which it has been signed at other stations, I think they should be regarded the same as the other officers who have signed it. But if the Officers at Hyderabad declined to sign in the manner described, that is without tagging a paper to the declaration as they have done already, there must be something faulty in their minds that must taint their allegiance, and while such a blot remains, there can be no cure.

You have now a decided opinion from me to which I can only add my hope that the officers at Hyderabad will consent to sign the Declaration under the same form simply observed at other Stations and that such act will be considered as sufficient to make them deserving of pardon.

You will of course write to me when Lord Minto arrives, and if leisure permits, keep me informed of the progress of measures, until tranquility and confidence be finally restored.

Yours, My dear Malcolm,
most truly,
B. CLOSE.

No. 20.

Secunderabad, 16 *Augt.* 1809.

MY DEAR RUMLEY,

We heard with much surprize and concern some Days ago of the removal of all the Officers from the Native Corps Cavalry and Infantry, at the Mount, in consequence of their having declined to sign the declaration tendered by Government. Whatever may be the views of Government in adopting this step, it must certainly be considered as a most impolitic one from the impression it must make on the minds of the Natives, and the subsequent Address or Proclamation to the Natives in the form of an Order by the Government in Council, translations of which in Hindoostanee have been industriously circulated among the Native Corps, cautioning them against ob... g their Officers, must inevitably prove such a shade (shock ?) to their Discipline and Subordination as will ultimately produce the most fatal consequences. It is a fact not to be controverted that the safety and prosperity of the British Empire in India depends upon the obedience and fidelity of the Native Troops, and it must be equally evident that their discipline and subordination in a great measure depends upon their obedience and attachment to and the confidence they place in their European Officers. The recent Order of the Governor in Council, if it has not entirely snapped these two asunder, will so materially injure and weaken them that the future existence of mutual confidence and attachment between the Natives and their Officers will be doubtful and precarious and their discipline might gradually be annihilated.

The late occurrences, at this place of resistance to the Orders of Government, you cannot be unacquainted with, and under that idea, I shall spare myself a detail of events which have given me more uneasiness and concern than anything that has before occurred during the whole course of my existence; however I may be implicated in the measures which have been adopted in that Force, I shall be consoled by an internal conviction that my influence and advice have been invariably exerted (however unsuccessful) to prevent all violent measures or resistance to the Orders of Government. I have felt in common with my Brother Officers a just sense of the injuries we have received, but in the consideration of an exertion for redress, I have never for a moment allowed myself to separate the interests and welfare of the Country with the furtherance of our cause.

Every man whose reason and reflection is not entirely swallowed up by the torrent of irritation and agitation which now prevails must shudder in contemplating the fatal calamities now impending and must feel an irresistible impulse to do all in his power to avert them. The Senior Officers of this Force under the influence of such feelings determined to make one effort which they conceived would greatly tend to the restoration of order and tranquility. On the 11th of this month they signed the Test or Declaration offered by Government, and after some difficulty succeeded in persuading all their Officers to do so. The same declaration thus signed, accompanied by a short address, was forwarded by express, on the morning of the 12th, to Lord Minto, and advices were immediately sent off to the different divisions of the Army, informing them of what we had done and earnestly exhorting them to follow our example, as the only step we considered now left to us to avert the dreadful calamities of a civil and unnatural warfare and prevent our being for ever severed from our Native Country. God grant that they may attend to our entreaties. India will yet be saved to the Mother country, and the Coast Army, by such a conspicuous proof of their patriotism, will effectually efface all the impressions occasioned by the late unfortunate excesses.

In our Address to Lord Minto, we make no demand, we leave everything to his decision, but earnestly intreat him to grant a General Amnesty for what has past. This Address will probably reach him immediately on his arrival. Such a proof of our confidence in him and the grateful reflection of so many Officers having returned to their allegiance must doubtless strengthen and improve any disposition he may possess for conciliating matters, and we may reasonably anticipate that, as a leading step towards tranquillity of the Army and renovating their confidence, he will be well disposed to acquiesce in our entreaty of granting a general Amnesty.

I enclose you the copy of a letter from Colonel Malcolm to a friend on the present situation of affairs. The arguments therein contained and the clear view that he has exhibited of the consequences of persevering in opposing Government must impress conviction on the mind of every man of the fatal and ruinous consequences which must inevitably be the result. This letter has made a great impression here, and I would wish you to give it all the publicity possible among the Officers who are with you. There can be little doubt but that the Jaulnah Force will immediately follow our example in signing the Declaration, and I most earnestly hope that those at Masulipatam and Seringapatam will be so induced, which will effectually terminate all the dreadful apprehensions which now prevail of the occurrence of a Civil Contest.

I have the pleasure to remain,
my dear Rumley, yours very sincerely,
GEO. NEALE.

Enclosure.—See No. 6.

No. 21.

Camp Woorgaum, August 17th, 1809.

MY DEAR NOBLE,

My mind is so distressed I can hardly put pen to paper. Since writing to you from Jaulna in reply to your Letter from Condittoor, circumstances have occurred which are scarcely credible to any honest man. We marched on the 14th from Jaulnah in the highest spirits. The Horse Artillery, Cavalry, and Flank Companies were then ordered to proceed from this place towards Hydrabad by rapid marches under Colonel D. We reached Portoor about the 15th, and on that night an express came from Hydrabad informing us that all that force had signed the test, had acknowledged their error and threw themselves on the mercy of Lord Minto: perfidious, weak men! A letter from Major Neale at the same time says—"If you have already moved from Jaulnah, march back again; your presence now is neither required nor wished for." I could not have conceived men such villains; a few days before, they were calling upon us to march and appeared to be ready to sacrifice their lives. This intelligence was a terrible blow to Colonel D. He at first determined to move on at all hazards, but changed his mind in the course of the night, and in the morning, while in expectation of moving off towards Hydrabad, the Colonel again addressed the men "that the officers whom we were going to support had signed the test, and as it would therefore be leading them to certain destruction by proceeding any farther, he had determined to lead them back to Jaulnah," and we retraced the ground which we had gone over with joy in our march and arrived at this place this morning with broken hearts. Our further conduct has not yet been determined on, but it is the wish of most to remain here till we get some intelligence from other parts of the Army, but

I much fear, my dear Noble, that we are degraded for ever by the infamous conduct of these men at Hydrabad. I have just received your Letter of the 31st despatched from Sadras, but it does not give us any satisfactory intelligence. We are still ready to sacrifice our lives in the Cause and we have every reason to believe the Native troops will stand by us, but we are so far removed from the rest of the Army that what we do one day may be counteracted the next in another quarter. I send you a copy of the Declaration of this Force upon our moving. It will, I think, show our moderation, and I am convinced that we should have carried our point had the Hydrabad Force held out. I am grieved to hear of the Ultimatum you mention; the *one* first drawn up was sent from Hydrabad to us for sanction and included the demands you mention, but which we viewed in the same light as you do, and drew up another which we were informed by the Hydrabad Committee was the one that was sent in; a copy of it accompanies and in which I conceive there is nothing which could have hurt the dignity of Government in complying with. There is certainly a want of system and communication with the different parts of the Army, but we are so scattered that this is impossible to arrange. Let the result now be what it may, the Service is ruined for ever. Lord Minto may, on his arrival, I think, see the absolute necessity of granting a General Amnesty in order to save the country from utter ruin. I do not think the flame is quite extinguished. If the test is offered here I do not think (if I can any longer trust in men) it will obtain a single signature. My mind is made up. I shall prefer begging my bread to swearing to serve the present Assassin, and I may therefore be with you yet at Pondicherry. At all events, when order is restored (and allowing the test is not proffered us), I shall apply to join the Battalion and prepare to quit the country; I can never remain with men whom I have been obliged in self-defence to bring in opposition to Government. I feel that I have hitherto acted openly and *honourably*, or rather according to the dictates of my heart. I shall have the satisfaction of thinking that I never took an oath to cut the throat of my dearest friend or brother-soldier, and which, I grieve to think, one of the best friends I had has done. It is too horrid to contemplate on the means Government have taken to subdue the Army; a pitiful victory it will be if they should succeed; all I have to regret is I have lost 9 of the best years of my life in a Service which I have endeavoured to support, I may say, with as much zeal as most officers in it, and am obliged to quit it penniless.

Jaulna 18th. We came in this morning. Had we proceeded, as was the wish of all the officers, we should have this day been at the Gateway, but the Colonel was determined that we should rest upon our arms here until we know what Lord Minto determines on. We yesterday heard that the Troops from Masulipatam have marched with the hope also of meeting with support from those men at Hydrabad. I send you a copy of a letter despatched to them, and similar letters will be forwarded to other parts of the

Army. Make the *one* I send you as public as possible. I had a letter from Morrison informing me of his having taken the test. It is too unpleasant a subject to comment on: I know not how to write to him. All desire to be affectionately remembered to you; pray, my dear Noble, write me often, it is the only consolation I shall have.

I am yours affectionately,

G. W. POIGNAND.

No. 22.

Bangalore, 18 *August*, 1809.

MY DEAR DICK,

I have this moment received yours of the 14th, announcing the sad news of your removal, which though sincerely lamented by us, does not much surprise, it was in fact what we dreaded. God above knows, my dear Friend, *when* we shall now meet. We had proposed setting off for Vellore, in the hope of passing a happy time in your company on the 20th, but now, as our friend is removed, we are undetermined and know not what to do; however, address my Letters to the friend you mention at Vellore, Dr. Jones; I shall write to him what to do with them, if we do not go down, yet I trust you have recommended us, or he will think me d—d impertinent.

I wrote you two days ago, transmitting what was reported as authentic news. From my heart, I rejoice to say that account was most erroneous; the *true* state of the case is this. The 1st Battalion 8th and 1st 15th having united, determined to push for Seringapatam. Above 30 miles from the Fort a body of Mysore horse appeared and soon began to annoy them, but our brave fellows held them in complete check upwards of 25 miles, when they were joined by a Squadron of the 25th Dragoons, under whose command is not said. Our friends hearing of their approach, pushed for the Fort, and when within two miles of it, *ran for it like the Devil.* Happily most of the Officers and about 700 men got safe in, 4 or 500 are prisoners, near 200 men killed or wounded. Captain Aiskell 15th is reported killed (I know not for certain that he is), Lieutenant Best of the 8th died of his wounds in Seringapatam. Captain McIntosh was wounded and taken prisoner. I have a letter saying he is in no danger, one wound in his Head and another in his hand. The Dragoons, to their honour, behaved most humanely, all the mischief was done by the Mysore force, *who cut up all they could.* I rejoice, my friend, this account is not so bloody as our first, but still hope *Vengeance will overtake the Man who caused even one drop of blood shed.* Lord Minto, I trust, will arrive in time to prevent any other sanguinary measures.

Lieutenant-Colonel Munro and Captain de Havilland had a Conference four miles from the Fort with Colonels Adams and Gibbs, the purport of course unknown, but they resolutely determine never to give up to Sir G. B., yet said when Lord Minto required them, they would surrender the Fort. This is right, it shews they are true to *their Allegiance*, that *the Man only is the object of disgust.* I trust nothing can prevent his speedy dismissal from Office. The report of Colonel Bell's suicide is a *most damnable lie* and the Villain ought to be d— who circulated it; he is a fine fellow and the admiration of all the Tollol de rida, Ah! Ah! Ah! Captain Nalp of the 59th Commanding *here* has this moment sent an order *for me to quit the Cantonment* this evening; it was delivered by an Officer who said I should be made Prisoner if I was found here in the morning!!! Mrs. H. is all hustle: "pack up" is the first word and "march" the second, so adieu, my ever dear Dick, accept of the best regard of "you know who" and ever believe me,

Your affectionate friend.

I believe I shall sign the test, if not, I shall not be allowed to go home. Say nothing.

No. 23.

Hyderabad, 19 *August*, 1809.

My dear Welsh,

I have been most anxiously looking for a letter from Nundrydrug till my patience is exhausted, and the Native reports from that quarter make me the more uneasy to hear what has become of you all. I will not offer any of my speculations on the subject, but as you may not know how matters stand here, will now inform you.

On the 3rd inst. Colonel Close arrived, harangued the Natives, who would not listen to him, and at length requested to be considered as a Prisoner, to which no one would agree. They afterwards had a meeting, and he promised to leave the Residency the next day, which he did. His report, I am told, was very handsome and as complimentary as was possible under circumstances of disobedience.

All went on smoothly for eight days with the exception of some jealousy between the King's and Company's Troops, afraid of each other. At length a consciousness of weakness, want of a Leader, fear of the Natives not standing by their Officers, and a sense of the danger that threatens the Country and the existence of our own dominion contributed to make the G.O. of the Governor-General particularly acceptable, as evincing a wish to reconcile the Government and the Army. It was, therefore, eagerly seized, as affording a proper opportunity to concede, and an address was resolved on to His Lordship. Many were drawn up, and after many days' discussion, was signed by all the Corps and forwarded. The Officers who signed this, at the same time volunteered to take the test, which they accordingly did. All seemed now in profound calm, altho' to me it appeared a deceitful one, when two days ago accounts arrived of Doveton's having at length resolved and put himself and whole force in motion to join this and the Masulipatam force. They marched on the 14th. Whether he will return, or prosecute his march, when he hears of the proceedings here are very doubtful. The Test was sent to me individually from the Adjutant-General's office and I instantly signed it. It is the counterpart of my Commission:

I could therefore have no hesitation in signing it *while I hold a Commission.* I must do as I promised by the test. When I refuse, I forfeit it. I hope you have signed it. Let me hear from you, I beg. A Rajah here wants a fine elephant. I have told him of yours. He wishes to know the price, his height, age, country and above all his cost. Give me a particular account of all these and I will try to sell him for ready money. If the Raja does not take, perhaps some other great man will. Remember me most particularly to Mrs. and Miss Welsh, who are well, I hope. Salams to all friends.

I received a letter from you of the 19th Ultimo, but I have waited in hopes of hearing what was become of you. Let me know all particulars of Nundy, Bangalore (where is Whyte ?) and Seringapatam.

Yours very faithfully,
S. MacDowall.

No. 24.

Malgotta. 29 *August*, 1809.

Dear Brother,

I received your letter previous to your leaving Wallajabad, and answered it immediately. I have not heard from you since. I shall now give you a short account of our unfortunate proceedings since we left the Droog, which was on the 5th August 1809. We arrived at Serah on the 7th, where it was necessary for our preservation to take 30 bullocks' load of rice, giving our receipt for the same. We proceeded without molestation until we arrived at Cuddapah, when the gates of the Fort were shut against us, in consequence of which we were obliged to move forward in order to procure forage, etc. in the next village. We had not marched more than two miles when we fell in with 3000 of Purniah's Horse, who sent one of their Chiefs to know what were our intentions. We told them that we were friends and did not come against them. They appeared satisfied, but still continued following us at a distance. In the evening we arrived at Naggamangalam and encamped, but could not procure any provisions as the Fort was shut and we did not like to force the Gates. At 10 p.m. the same day we moved on for Seringapatam, and had arrived within ten miles of that place, when, to our surprise and astonishment, several followers and sepoys from a small village in our rear came to us desperately wounded. We immediately took precautions against such treachery on ourselves and continued our march, *now* surrounded by the whole of the Horse, who continued firing upon us from all quarters. Several times they attempted to charge but were always driven back. As almost the whole of our baggage had been plundered in the rear, we resolved to push on for Seringapatam without delay, and would have arrived at that place in safety had not the 59th and 25th Dragoons intercepted us when within 4 miles of Seringapatam. We immediately struck off to the right in order to save ourselves from being *entirely* surrounded by them, and made for a Nulla in front which the Grenadiers had made, when the 25th and Purneah's Horse cut in among us. Here I must tell you that we had marched 70 miles in the 24 hours, and halted only 4 hours during that period. You may suppose how tired our "poor men" must have been, indeed a great many from fatigue were in the rear, and when the Dragoons came down, there were not 800 men in the two Battalions, and they, poor fellows, seeing such an immense force coming against them, threw down their arms and made for the Nullah. Now commenced a most inhuman butchery by the Dragoons and Mysore Horse. They did not even spare women and children, several of whom were murdered in a Bungalow they had taken shelter in. By a most singular good fortune, every Officer escaped except Captain Mackintosh, who was wounded and taken to Mysore. Luckily for him, he exchanged caps with Degraves, which undoubtedly saved his life, for his own was a thin cap and the one he had from Degraves was four skins thick and a thick lining inside, all of which were cut through; they likewise cut through a thick neckcloth, and wounded him slightly. Best, of ours, fell from his horse, and partly from the blow, and fatigue during the day, died in the night. Our casualties are few considering the immense number of troops against us. We had taken 30 and 40 killed and 180 wounded and some missing. I give you my word this is all true, which you will be a little surprised at after reading the account in the paper, which is one continued series of lies.

Most of the men that were brought in are desperately wounded, some having ten and eleven wounds. Several of them said the Dragoons' officers amused themselves by cutting at them when wounded on the ground. I suppose that was in order to try their dexterity.

You know of course Seringapatam was given up a few days ago. Tho' the Corps separated we were ordered to Malgottah, 18 miles off, where we are at present waiting for further orders. All our officers are anxious to know how affairs will terminate. It is greatly to be lamented that we did not receive the letters from Mr. Cole and Colonel Davis which I understand they sent yesterday as not to proceed. Even had an officer come to us from either of the King's Corps informing us of the consequences in case we did come, or we should never have proceeded.

Yours

JAS. BAKER.

I lost everything except my Horse, amounting in value to me 585 pagodas.

No. 25.

Noymongol on the Chittledroog Road.
31st August, 1809.

MY DEAR CRISP,

I do not see your name in the list of those who have signed the Declaration. It being exactly the tenor of your Commission, I am at a loss to think why you can *deliberately* refuse to sign it, for I consider many who have refused did so merely because others did. "The few led the many." I will answer a question which I suppose you will ask, before you put it to me, "Why I myself did not." I have now; I could not before, as I was in a manner a Prisoner in the Fort of Seringapatam; those on the outside would not let me out and those in the inside would have been glad to get rid of me. I will tell you the whole story, which is now too long to write, when I see you next. If you refused the Declaration, send in your signature immediately; you need not speak of having done it, all the officers here, when they found themselves obliged to give up the Fort, signed it as their last resource. There is now no reason for any longer declining it. All at Hyderabad have done the same.

Instead of ordering me away with the Corps, as the others were, Colonel Davis, convinced how little I had to say in all that went forward, has directed me to go to Chittledroog, where I shall command. I think there will be a severe example made of those who marched from that place and of the leaders in Seringapatam. Take my advice, say nothing about it, sign immediately. You may be sure all your Corps will.

When I am certain where you are, I will write more particularly. I have much more to tell you than I can write.

Believe me, my dear Crisp, yours sincerely,

T. S. Williams.

INDEX OF NAMES

INDEX OF NAMES